ON OF TABLETS HUMAN HEARTS

ON TABLETS OF HUMAN HEARTS

CHRISTIAN EDUCATION WITH CHILDREN

MARY ELLEN DRUSHAL

ZondervanPublishingHouse

Academic and Professional Books

Grand Rapids, Michigan

A Division of HarperCollinsPublishers

On Tablets of Human Hearts
Copyright © 1991 by Mary Ellen Drushal

Requests for information should be addressed to:
Zondervan Publishing House
Academic and Professional Books
1415 Lake Drive S.E.
Grand Rapids, Michigan 49506

Library of Congress Cataloging-in-Publication Data

On tablets of human hearts : Christian education with children /
Mary Ellen Drushal.
    p.   cm.
Includes bibliographical references and index.
ISBN 0-310-36840-5 (alk. paper)
1. Christian education of children.   I. Title.
BV1475.2.D74   1991
268'.432–dc20   90-43943
                                                                      CIP

Edited by Susan Lutz and Jan M. Ortiz
Designed by Jan M. Ortiz

Printed in the United States of America

91 92 93 94 95 96 / DH / 10 9 8 7 6 5 4 3 2 1

This edition is printed on acid-free paper and meets the American National Standards
Institute Z39.48 standard.

This book is dedicated to all the people
who have cheered me on:

MY FAMILY
(especially Mike, Lori, Jeff, Dad, Mom, and Alice),

MY BUDDY
(Morven),

MY DEAREST FRIENDS
(Barb, Kay, Syd, Meredith, Holly, Jerry, Fred, Doug,
Judy, and Diane),

MY FORMER TEACHERS
(Ima, Ray, Betty, Liz, Earline, Kent, and Kathy),

AND ALL THE CHILDREN WHO HAVE TAUGHT ME.

THANK YOU.

CONTENTS

List of Figures   11
Preface   13
Introduction   15
    Creating a Learning Environment
    The Goal of Our Instruction
    God's Unconditional Love

PART I. UNDERSTANDING THE LEARNING PROCESS

Chapter 1.   Listening Initiates Learning   27
      Listening
      Biblical Principles
      Practical Application
      Educational Foundation for Practical
        Application

Chapter 2.   First-Hand Explorers Learn More   45
      Exploring
      Biblical Principles
      Practical Application
      Educational Foundation for Practical
        Application

Chapter 3.   "Seek and Ye Shall Find"   61
      Discovering
      Biblical Principles
      Practical Application
      Educational Foundation for Practical
        Application

Chapter 4.   Internalizing Truth   75
      Appropriating
      Biblical Principles
      Practical Application

                   Educational Foundation for Practical
                    Application

Chapter 5.   Life-Changing Behavior   89
                  Assuming Responsibility
                  Biblical Principles
                  Practical Application
                  Educational Foundation for Practical
                    Application

PART II: TEACHING EFFECTIVELY IN THE CLASSROOM

Chapter 6.   Influences on Classroom Environment   103
                  Acquiring a Biblical Self-Image
                  Accepting a Biblical Self-Image
                  Effective Teacher Characteristics
                  Planning Effective Lessons
                  Preparing Effective Lessons

Chapter 7.   Teaching for Learning Styles   121
                  The Learner's Role
                  The Role of the Effective Teacher
                  Learning Styles and the Learning Process

Chapter 8.   —Assisting the Child's Personal Development   133
                  Emotional Development
                  Spiritual Development
                  Physical Development
                  Intellectual Development
                  Social Development

Chapter 9.   Managing the Classroom   147
                  Discipline
                  Evaluation
                  Cooperation vs. Competition in the Classroom

Chapter 10.   Administering Children's Programs   163
                  Ministering as Jesus Did
                  Delineate the Purpose, Goals, and Objectives of
                    the Program
                  Select a Target Group of Children
                  Scheduling the Time
                  Plan the Schedule for Each Day
                  Evaluate the Effectiveness of the New Program

PART III: RELIEVING CHILDHOOD STRESS

Chapter 11.   Working in Tandem with the Home   177
    Dealing with Children in Transition
    Loss and Separation
    Losses of Another Kind
    Adult Problems That Affect Children

PART IV: PURSUING EXCELLENCE IN CHILDREN'S MINISTRY

Chapter 12.   Responding to God's Call   197
    Feed My Lambs
    Take Care of My Sheep
    Feed My Sheep
    Pursuing Excellence After Responding to
      God's Call
    Differences Between Teaching and Educating

Chapter 13.   Meeting the Needs of All Children   207
    Children Need to Know
    Be Goal-Oriented
    Children Will Not Always Be As They Are

Index   221

LIST OF FIGURES

1. Contemporary Approaches to Christian Education   18
2. The Learning Process (Listening)   29
3. Components of Educational Theories   34
4. An Outline of Proficient Listening   37
5. Listening Model   38
6. The Learning Process (Exploring)   46
7. Sequence of Cognitive Structures   54–55
8. The Learning Process (Discovering)   62
9. Dale's Cone of Learning   64
10. The Learning Process (Appropriating)   76
11. The Learning Process (Assuming Responsibility)   90
12. Erikson's Eight States of Man   95
13. The Complete 4MAT System Model   122
14. Meshing Learning Styles With the Learning Process   127
15. The Childhood Years in Erikson's Stages of Life   134
16. Fowler's Stages of Faith   138
17. Glasser's Strategy for Maintaining Discipline   149
18. Criteria for Selection of Curriculum   156
19. Contrasts Between Teachers and Educators   200–201
20. A Unique Wheelbarrow   211

PREFACE

God is in the habit of giving us wonderful gifts. One is our children. Another is eternal life, which often begins in childhood. We are born in all shapes, sizes, and colors, but with one commonality: each of us is created in God's image, just as he intended.

That image within each of us is subtly molded, not only by our own inner nature, but by our experiences and contacts with others. Every event, situation, and personal encounter we have is mentally recorded; each has an impact on the adult personalities and perspectives that will be ours someday. Thus children and adults are sojourners in life together, and their interactions with one another leave indelible messages on the tablets of human hearts around them (2 Cor. 3:3). The marks impressed upon our own hearts will be exposed as we allow others to know us.

As children's personalities are formed and their informal educational pursuits begin, there are ways that adults can leave helpful, positive messages on the tablets of their hearts; impressions that will assist rather than impede a child's development. This book outlines some of the ways adults can accomplish this. It is meant to be a tool for those who desire to minister to children. It seeks to introduce the Christian educator to the various disciplines that determine the way adults perceive the purpose, context, and content of children's ministry. The goal of this book is to provide information that will create an enthusiasm for children's ministry, that will impel one to pursue excellence in planning programs for children. A list of resources is included at the end of each chapter to encourage further study.

Christian educators can provide quality experiences that help children become confident, competent, and ultimately spiritual adults. But to accomplish this, we must understand how children think, how they learn, and what situations in life cause them stress and pain. Christian educators must have a working knowledge of child development—intellectual, social, emotional, spiritual, and physical.

13

Armed with such knowledge, educators can design stimulating and creative learning environments and also learn to effectively teach children.

During the fifteen years that I have planned and conducted programs for children, I have involved them, questioned them, and observed them in study and in play. Training and interacting with their teachers and parents has also shaped my views of children's ministry. I have concluded that teachers teach the way they were taught and parents parent the way they were parented unless some conscious decisions are made to accomplish these tasks in other ways. I hope this text will challenge your thinking and cause you to evaluate the importance of interacting with children. I hope that it will give you the insight and courage to implement some alternative approaches to ministry with them.

Educators in the church need to understand both educational theory and biblical principles in order to provide quality Christian education experiences for God's children. It is my hope that this book will help you to discover new ways to apply these truths to the educational experiences you offer the children in your care; to their ultimate spiritual benefit.

Thanks be to God.

Mary Ellen Drushal, Ph.D.
Associate Professor of Christian Education
and Church Administration

INTRODUCTION

Imagine you are enrolled in a class. As you enter the room you notice there is a question written on the chalkboard. Take your seat and begin to contemplate the question: *What do children need?*

What do children need?	

A question always demands a response and as the class participates, the board is soon full of answers:

What do children need?		
attention	love	
security	health	
to be listened to		
discipline	caring	
laughter	friends	
affirmation	exercise	

The teacher has purposely left space for an additional question and then adds it to the board for your consideration: *What do adults need?*

What do children need?		What do adults need?	
attention	love	love	attention
security	health	friends	security
to be listened to		to be listened to	
discipline	caring	exercise	health
laughter	friends	laughter	self-
affirmation	exercise		discipline

The interesting thing is that adults need the same things that children need. Adult needs may have a different order of priority, but

15

they are basically the same as children's. Theorists once wrote about children as if they were miniature adults. The reality is the reverse: adults are grown-up children with precisely the same needs!

If this is true, then learning to teach children effectively should not be an insurmountable obstacle for adults. The only thing teachers require is an understanding of their own needs in order to minister to children.

Just as the needs of children and adults are alike, spiritual questions are somewhat the same as well. "Who is this guy Jesus?" "How can Jesus be Jesus, God, and the Holy Spirit all at one time?" "What does it mean to have Jesus in my heart?"[1] These questions, while posed by children, are ones that adults must also answer, not only for themselves but for the children in their care. The seriousness with which we, as adults, respond to children's questions, what we say, and how we say it should be the essence of our teaching.

Who is this guy Jesus anyway? Adults have a distinct advantage over young children. They can read and study Scripture for themselves, discover who Jesus is, learn of his impact in history, and begin to realize how he designs the future for his children—grown or still growing. But who fully knows Jesus?

How can Jesus be Jesus, God, and the Holy Spirit all at one time? How many adults really understand the abstract concept of the Trinity? Moreover, who is able to explain the interrelationships of these three Persons to a child? Or should children even try to contemplate this complex doctrine?

What does it mean to have Jesus in my heart? Do adults fully comprehend the realities of this intimate relationship with God? It is difficult to understand that he loved us so much that he came to earth to rescue us from our sin.

Children ask these kinds of weighty questions. The challenge to adults interacting with children is how to respond to them with the wisdom and sensitivity the questions—and the children—deserve.

Can children arrive at an understanding of who Jesus is, appreciate the complexities of the Trinity, and receive the gift of salvation so freely offered? Yes, they can, if adults will spend quality time with them to: build relationships, introduce concepts at appropriate developmental levels, explain concepts in language children use and understand, offer time and opportunities for learning activities that reinforce what is to be learned and felt, and trust the Holy Spirit to be the ultimate teacher. Nurturing children in this way is a distinct privilege. It requires more than the ability to tell a Bible story well enough to keep the attention of any number of squirming children for sixty minutes![2]

Children can grow in faithfulness to God and in Christlikeness if adults take them seriously, show respect for them and their unique learning capabilities, and "train them in the way they should go . . ." (Prov. 22:6). Discipleship begins early, and the foundation must be established very firmly if it is to endure for a lifetime.[3]

For a moment consider the list of terms mentioned that are related to children: questioning/responding, teaching, nurturing, faithfulness, Christlikeness, the Trinity, salvation, and training in discipleship. Can all of this really be accomplished with children? Yes. But teachers need to be trained to listen to children's verbal and nonverbal language, to understand how children learn, and then to apply that knowledge, thus becoming more effective encouragers of children.

The remainder of this book will explore the ways that children learn, the ways that effective teaching is based upon our knowledge of the learning process, and ways to orient our adult selves to the child's view of the world. As a first step, we must consider various approaches to Christian education for children.

Christian education ministries are organized around many different theological perspectives. We need to be familiar with the main schools of thought so that we know how our own views would be categorized. Figure 1 presents five contemporary approaches to Christian education. In examining my own biblical roots, my educational background, and my practical experience, I find that my views fit most naturally in the "Spiritual Development" and "Interpretation" categories. My classroom instruction focuses on the whole child, on how the child ascribes meaning to experiences, and on how the individual is shaped and guided through the interaction of Scripture with culture and life. "To be beloved by, and to belove the Christian experience embodied in the redemptive community, is the beginning of Christian education."[4]

> Study Figure 1 to determine which approach most nearly reflects your personal views or goals, the role of teacher and child, and the content and setting for learning.

Our approach to Christian education is defined by Whose we are, Whom we serve, and how we view our role and responsibility for those we nurture. That is, what we actually do in the classroom is a product of our biblical theology (our understanding of Whose we are and Whom we serve), and our educational philosophy of ministry (how we see our educational role and responsibility). These perspectives will shape our goals and practice in the classroom. The soundness of these underlying assumptions and the degree of creativ-

Figure 1
Seymour & Miller
Contemporary Approaches To Christian Education[5]

	Religious Instruction	Faith Community	Spiritual Development	Liberation	Interpretation
Goals	to transmit Christian religion (understandings and practice)	to build the congregation into a community where persons can encounter the faith and learn its life-style	to enable persons to grow in faith to spiritual maturity	to transform the church and persons for liberation and humanization	to connect Christian perspectives and practices to contemporary experiences
View of Teacher	structurer of a learning environment	priest for the community	spiritual director or sponsor	colleague	guide
View of Learner	learner with developmental and personal needs and interests	person struggling to identify with the Christian community; congregation seeking to be faithful	person moving through stages of development to maturity	both "Christian" persons and groups	person seeking to interpret Christianity and experience
Content	Christian religion	Christian community's faith and life-style	Christian faith	critical reflection on life-style in light of Christian faith	Christian story and present experience
Settings for Learning	primarily formal educational settings	community of faith	person's total life	places where Christians are involved in the world	person's total life
Curriculum	teacher structures the learning environment to enable the learner to acquire Christian religion	priest enables congregation to seek to be faithful and exposes "catechumens" to learning points in the community of faith	spiritual director nurtures a person through significant life crises to grow in faith	persons dialogue about their lives so as to bring to awareness structures of power, alternatives for society, and actions for transformation	guide helps persons understand the meaning of experience in relation to the Christian story.
Contribution	serious attention to the application of educational research to the church	increased awareness of the community nature of the Christian church and its educational settings	definition of the ways faith grows in children and adults	concern with the church's mission and involvement in issues of social justice and societal transformation	emphasis placed on discovering relationships among Christian faith. God's present activity, and contemporary experience
Problems	expectation of a higher level of professionalism than may be present in church setting; biased toward more formal educational settings and learning of content	difficulty of intentionally using enculturation structures; apparent assumption that a church community is faithful	difficulty of assessing stages of development; overemphasis on the individual	difficulty of dealing with power and change in the church	difficulty of actually doing theological reflection on experience

ity with which we implement them in the classroom will determine the effectiveness of the teaching/learning experience.

CREATING A LEARNING ENVIRONMENT

The physical design of the classroom plays an important part in a child's learning experience. But there is another element that is central to an optimal learning environment, totally unrelated to the physical surroundings of the classroom. That element is the **teacher.**

Christian education programs in churches are usually staffed by volunteer teachers (some more willing and able than others). The teacher in the classroom affects learning by affirming or denying some intangible realities of the Christian life. The teacher can have both positive and negative influences on the learning environment. A teacher may desire to teach God's Word and have the finest equipment, curriculum materials, and teaching plan possible, and yet fail to communicate adequately. Even teachers need teachers. It is the responsibility of Christian educators (in church and college settings) to train and equip the volunteer teachers for ministry (Eph. 4:12).

If we assume that we have a facility that has been appropriately designed and equipped, and that we have teachers who earnestly desire to teach and communicate God's Word to children and who have been trained for the task, what else must be considered in creating a learning environment? The facets of Christian education that follow are intangible elements, but they have a powerful influence on the learning environment.

THE GOAL OF OUR INSTRUCTION

Adults should have a passion for teaching that results in changed lives.[6] Besides a knowledge of Scripture and a reason for choosing to teach children, we should know what we hope to accomplish through the power of the Holy Spirit.

As Christian teachers our goal, along with Paul the great apostle of the faith, is "We proclaim him, admonishing and teaching everyone with all wisdom, so that we may present everyone perfect in Christ" (Col. 1:28). What a tall order for Christian teachers and educators—to teach children and train adult teachers with "all wisdom" and in such a way as to encourage their growth, development, and understanding so that they ultimately become "complete," "perfect," and "mature" in Christ.

As teachers we are to be wise—to make use of all we know about Scripture, our own relationship with Jesus Christ, our knowledge of child development, learning, teaching, and communication. In addition, we must exercise the good judgment that comes to us as we receive and accept the mind of Christ. Children and adults must learn that we are created in God's image to pursue a holy life of spiritual growth. Nurturing or teaching children is an interactive and intentional process. "The spiritual person and the spiritual community are both agents of formation, but they accomplish this formation most completely when there is a conscious effort to assist individuals in the development of the spiritual life."[7]

The goal of assisting children in pursuing wholeness in Christ must be accompanied by a comprehension of God's unconditional love for humanity.

GOD'S UNCONDITIONAL LOVE

Every person born into this world is a sojourner who occupies a brief period in time. Scripture frequently reminds us that we are mere shadows and vapors upon this earth, and yet God chose to accomplish his ministry through people like us, we who were all one time children. The fact that he loves his creation unconditionally should not be surprising to those who know Scripture and yet, because of our sinful nature, it seems incomprehensible.

> He saved us, not because of righteous things we had done, but because of his mercy. He saved us through the washing of rebirth and renewal by the Holy Spirit, whom he poured out on us generously through Jesus Christ our Savior, so that, having been justified by his grace, we might become heirs having the hope of eternal life. (Titus 3:5–7)

What a promise is ours!

God's unconditional love is the basis for our salvation. He loved us so much he sent his only Son to die for us (John 3:16). God loves us supremely, like no one else ever can.[8] Being loved because of our creation in God's image and being redeemed from sin through the ultimate loving act—Jesus' death on the cross—demands a response from us. "Be imitators from God, therefore, as dearly loved children, and live a life of love, just as Christ loved us and gave himself up for us as a fragrant offering and sacrifice to God" (Eph. 5:1–2). We respond as we imitate God and make his love manifest in society. "Love wills the good of all and never wills harm or evil to any."[9] We also respond as we receive the gift of salvation and live a life of obedience to Christ's call for service.

> For the grace of God that brings salvation has appeared to all men. It teaches us to say "No" to ungodliness and worldly passions, and to live self-controlled, upright and godly lives in this present age, while we wait for the blessed hope—the glorious appearing of our great God and Savior, Jesus Christ, who gave himself for us to redeem us from all wickedness and to purify for himself a people that are his very own, eager to do what is good. These, then, are the things you should teach. Encourage and rebuke with all authority. Do not let anyone despise you. (Titus 2:11–15)

What hope and instruction is available to others as we live as God's representatives to this world!

As Christian educators we must know we are created in God's image, that we have been redeemed through Christ, and that we are therefore loved unconditionally, absolutely, and without reservation. Without that personal and experiential knowledge, we have nothing to teach. We are to teach Scripture because it is the only thing that will last forever (Isa. 40:8) and because "all Scripture is God-breathed and is useful for teaching, rebuking, correcting and training in righteousness, so that the man of God may be thoroughly equipped for every good work" (2 Tim. 3:16–17).

Christian education's ultimate hope for children is that they know and love God and serve him with a deep commitment forever. The focus of each class session should be shaped by this goal. It should evolve from a consideration of the child's developmental stage, the biblical truth being taught, and the opportunities for participation in as many sensory experiences as possible. We can trust God for the work of regeneration in our children's lives as we endeavor to educate them in meaningful ways.

We are all sojourners involved in this pilgrimage of faith in Christian education. The fundamental goal for children is to receive the gift of salvation and to be nurtured and discipled into faith, trust, and growth toward maturity with Christ. Christian education means "to live content."[10] If children are to believe and practice their faith in real life, they need parents and teachers who live their lives in honest, open interaction with the living God and with other people. Deuteronomy 6:4–7 describes this dynamic, daily-living model of interaction, utilizing every teachable moment to internalize a love for God. This was not one option out of many for parents. God commanded instruction in this way, and then underscored the need for modeling by sending his Son to live life before the watching world. Christ is the master teacher.[11] He stands not only as a living example for teachers but his ministry also illustrates the kinds of learning experiences we need to provide for children in our churches today.

"The most significant development among evangelicals in recent years is the growing awareness that Christian nurture must happen in a dynamic, integral, and transactional way within the church as the body of Christ."[12] As sojourners who have entered into the body of Christ, children and adults together need to sense the awe and love of the Creator, and to appreciate the uniqueness with which each is created. We also need the long-term view that someday we will all be together in heaven to experience eternity with God Almighty. This experience is described in a children's classic this way: "If ever I do Inherit Eternity that my Children will be there, just beyond the Enchanted Door, awaiting The Great Magician. And that when He doth appear, then shall we behold the greatest Magic of all: The Miracle of Immortality!"[13]

Christian education and nurture does not occur, as Humphreys outlines, through magic. We are educating for eternity, and it is plain hard work—rewarding and exciting work with eternal results. There is more to teaching than telling a Bible story. More is involved in learning than hearing the Word. Learning to teach effectively comes as a result of personal, conscious, and intentional decision-making in designing quality, stimulating, and creative Christian educational experiences for children.

ENDNOTES

[1]Gayle von Keyserling, Unpublished Master's Project, "Devotional Literature for Children" (Ashland, Ohio: Ashland Theological Seminary, 1988).

[2]Lawrence O. Richards, *A Theology of Children's Ministry* (Grand Rapids: Zondervan, 1983).

[3]Colleen Townsend Evans, *Teaching Your Child to Pray* (New York: Doubleday & Co., 1978), and Wes Haystead, *Teaching Your Child About God: You Can't Begin Too Soon* (Ventura, Calif.: Regal, 1974).

[4]Jack L. Seymour and Donald E. Miller, *Contemporary Approaches to Christian Education* (Nashville: Abingdon, 1982), 130.

[5]Ibid., 32–33. Used by permission of the editor, Perry LeFevre.

[6]Howard G. Hendricks, *Teaching to Change Lives* (Portland, Ore.: Multnomah Press, 1987).

[7]Iris V. Cully, *Education for Spiritual Growth* (San Francisco: Harper & Row, 1984), 31.

[8]Anthony A. Hoekema, *Created in God's Image* (Grand Rapids: Zondervan, 1986).

[9]A. W. Tozer, *The Knowledge of the Holy* (New York: Harper & Row, 1961), 105.

[10]Robert E. Webber, *Common Roots: A Call to Evangelical Maturity* (Grand Rapids: Zondervan, 1978), 189.

[11]Gayle D. Erwin, *The Jesus Style* (Waco, Tex.: Word, 1983), and Edward Kulhman, *Master Teacher* (Old Tappan, N.J.: Revell, 1987).

[12]Webber, *Common Roots*, 190.

[13]Alice Lee Humphreys, *Angels in Pinafores* (Richmond, Va.: John Knox, 1954), 93.

PART I

Understanding the Learning Process

To teach effectively, adults must first examine how learners learn. Through the exploration of Scripture and significant educational theories, the Christian educator can begin to determine *why* we do what we do in the classroom.

Part I provides an introductory glimpse of educational theory and practice. Much more study will be necessary for one to acquire a thorough understanding of the discipline of Christian education. The information contained in this section, therefore, looks at only the tip of the iceberg in educational theory and should not be viewed as a comprehensive review of the literature described.

It is important for teachers to understand contemporary educational theories so that in the Christian education classroom, children will learn to understand their role and influence in the world.

> The learning that is of most worth enables us to get a sense of our individual and social identity—who we are, what we care about, and what we can do. This self-analysis tells us whether we are in charge of our own lives or are ruled by others, an actor or a spectator, powerful or weak, a manager or managed. It tells us whether we believe the world can be changed or whether change is impossible.[1]

Change is possible in our teaching habits.

If change is consciously pursued, it can result in more effective learning and teaching. To that end, and building upon the foundation laid in this section, there is a list of resources at the end of each chapter that can offer a more comprehensive exposure to researchers and their theories.

Chapter 1

Listening Initiates Learning

This is a book written for Christians who are teaching children and want to become more effective in their teaching ministry. Like the children they teach, teachers come in various shapes, sorts, and sizes, and bring with them personal abilities and sets of experiences that have molded their behavior and expectations. Some teachers are more effective in the classroom than others. Much research literature has been produced on the topic of effective teaching in the classroom, and a variety of opinions exist on proper student-teacher relationships and classroom management. But all agree that a prerequisite for effective teaching is an understanding of the learning process and the various functions of each element—teachers, learners, innate abilities, parents, environment, and motivations for learning.

Next to the significant relationship between parents, children are the most valuable and tangible product of a marriage. Scripture tells us to be fruitful and multiply (Gen. 1:22 KJV) and the Psalmist says that children are a blessing from the Lord. "Sons are a heritage from the LORD, children a reward from him. Like arrows in the hands of a warrior are sons born in one's youth. Blessed is the man whose quiver is full of them. They will not be put to shame when they contend with their enemies in the gate" (Ps. 127:3–5). Along with having children, however, comes a tremendous responsibility; that of training them in the way they should go (Prov. 22:6).

In the Jewish tradition recorded in Deuteronomy 6:4–7, the family was clearly the single most important influence in a child's training. Through their intimate relationship, parents were instructed to teach their children *diligently* while walking together, preparing to sleep, sitting down for a meal, and in all other facets of normal family activity.

In modern days, these "teachable moments" occur when families are together riding in the car, shopping at the mall, strolling the beach, and even visiting an amusement park or an art museum. Parents are to be with their children and teach them *diligently* about things of the kingdom, to explain what Scripture says regarding the desires, values, and behavior we are to display as believers in the Lord Jesus Christ. Parents are to model Christ. Children absorb the training of their parents and God has promised that "when [they are] old [they] will not turn from it" (Prov. 22:6). In this way, parents perpetuate the kingdom with a new generation whose worldview reflects their calling as servants of the Lord Christ.

Some parents think of their children as clay pots for whose shaping and molding they hold responsibility. This is a biblical image, used by Isaiah when he described humanity as the clay and God as the Potter (Isa. 64:8). The molded clay pot is placed in a kiln to be fired and hardened into usefulness. What parents need to remember is that there is no magical transformation process that takes place in the kiln. The pot emerges with the same structural quality it had going into the kiln; it is just harder and sturdier.

A porcelain vase, which is also made from clay, is created in much the same way as clay pots except that the beginning material is of a finer quality and the craftsman has spent more hours preparing the ingredients for firing. When the kiln is opened, a valuable, beautiful, and translucent porcelain vase is a reality. The vase is not mystically transmogrified during the firing process; the ultimate product is heavily dependent on the original quality of the clay and the time invested by the artisan who molded and shaped it.

There are parallels here to the process of rearing and teaching children. Children of porcelain quality emerge from homes and classrooms where parents and teachers have spent the necessary hours in preparing the clay. Children of porcelain quality emerge when they have enjoyed the kinds of learning experiences that prepare them to endure the fires of life.

Therefore, the life experiences we provide our children must be carefully designed. Parents and teachers need to be aware of both ancient and recent discoveries regarding children. Their parenting and teaching should reflect conscious decisions to do what is best for the child, so that when the child is fully trained and ready to undertake the tasks God has directed, his or her life is of a quality sufficient for the tasks.

As the church through Christian education assists parents and teachers in this developmental process, it must first help them understand how learning takes place.

Figure 2 is a visual model of the learning process. We will examine each component of the learning process and, in Part II of this text, we will explore what impact our teaching has on learning.

Figure 2
The Learning Process[2]
(Listening)

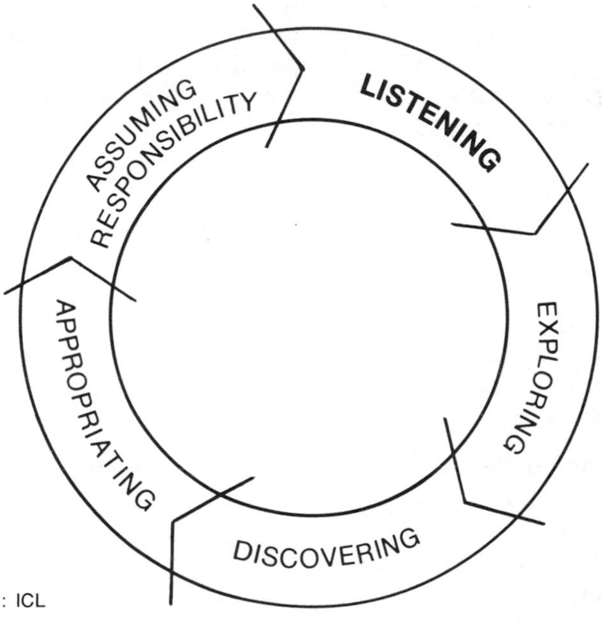

Ventura, Calif.: ICL

LISTENING

All learning begins with some form of **listening.** Listening activates the mind and commences thinking. Speech, language, and reading are learned and developed as the child listens to and then imitates the sounds. Social behavior is learned as the child listens and watches significant others at home and at play. The acceptance of Christian principles also comes through listening.

Christian educators bring a spiritual dimension to the educational process. A test of their scholarship is to evaluate educational truths and research according to Scripture. If Scripture is truth and is the standard for faith, practice, judgment, and excellence, then educational theory and practice must be judged through the biblical grid. God has created people with minds and hearts with which to discern biblical truths and to evaluate research and its educational implications for children in Scripture's light. Therefore, let us consider biblical evidence, both direct and implied, as we examine the component of listening in the learning process.

Biblical Principles

James 1:5 states: "If any of you lacks wisdom, he should ask God, who gives generously to all without finding fault, and it will be given to him." As we ask and listen, God will respond. Young children are eager to absorb all their environment has to offer. Jesus said, "If anyone has ears to hear, let him hear" (Mark 4:23).

We must listen to the truth of Scripture if we are to live obedient lives in this present world. Second Corinthians 10:4–5 reminds us that:

> the weapons we fight with are not the weapons of the world. On the contrary, they have divine power to demolish strongholds. We demolish arguments and every pretension that sets itself up against the knowledge of God, and we take captive every thought to make it obedient to Christ.

If learners are to become critical thinkers and not mere parrots of culture, then listening is necessary to comprehend the points made in any argument or debate.

The listening component of the learning process implies a teacher-oriented function. This is the format for the traditional classroom: the teacher is active while the learner is passive. The teacher instructs and the students listen to learn. This model has truth in it; however, teachers should not make the assumption that listening is all that is required for the student to learn. The learning process depicted in Figure 2 suggests that this concept is a myth. Before learners can experience long-term learning, they must be encouraged and guided through the entire learning process, which requires active participation on the part of the learner.

A classroom where learners are actively involved allows the learning process to function optimally. True learning has not been accomplished until the behavior has changed. (Note the last phase of the learning process in Figure 2, which is assuming responsibility.) The role of the teacher in the listening phase of the learning process is to encourage the learners and guide them into the next phase of the learning process to see what biblical truth and understanding awaits.

Volunteer teachers frequently conduct their classes in the traditional manner: only telling or lecturing. They expect that if learners listen, they will automatically assume responsibility for behavioral change. You will notice in Figure 2 that listening and assuming responsibility are only two components of the learning process. Without experiencing the other components that lie in between, only short-term learning can be expected.

The following story, using the adult concept of tithing, illustrates how easily learning is extinguished when the entire learning process is not completed.

> Follow the components of the learning process (Figure 2) as they are revealed in this illustration.

A church was deeply committed to sending fifty percent of its annual budget to support missionary efforts around the world. To encourage liberality in giving, they brought in a speaker for a missions conference who was noted for his ability to "loosen the purse strings" of adult believers. He spoke on five evenings, each time presenting a message from Scripture that could not be refuted. At the conclusion of the conference, missions giving increased to record levels, but within three months, the giving returned to its pre-conference level.

The church had made the basic assumption that learners listen and assume responsibility for changed behavior. Increased giving for only three months exemplifies the short-term learning that takes place when the learning process is not complete.

The saga continues. The second year a missions conference was held, the elders of the church decided to apply the principles of the learning process, because they deeply desired this church to receive the long-term blessing that is a part of a significant ministry to remote parts of the earth (Acts 1:8). Again, a speaker presented a series of irrefutable messages from Scripture on presenting the tithe to the church. The difference this time came after the lectures. The people were invited to enjoy some refreshments and then to proceed to small discussion groups where trained leaders guided them into exploring the Scripture that had been the focus for the evening. In these sessions, adult learners began to center upon the Word of God, and *explore* and *discover* the biblical truths for themselves. They had the opportunity to interact with others and to raise questions. They had the time needed for the learning process to be completed, which in this instance would lead them to personally own the biblical truth (*appropriate*) and *assume responsibility* for tithing their income for the ministry of the church.

At the conclusion of the second year of the missions conference, this church accomplished its goal of achieving sustained missionary support through tithes and offerings, but only after church leaders respected the learners sufficiently enough to guide them through the complete learning process. Mere listening will not necessarily lead a person to assume responsibility for the truth taught. When the learner experiences every phase of the learning process, however, long-term learning is the result.

Learners need to be led by teachers through the complete learning process if long-term learning and behavioral change is the goal. Teachers, therefore, need to teach in such a way as to motivate the learner toward completing the learning process. By using a variety of teaching tools, methodologies, and styles, a teacher can assist the learner in exploring the biblical truth.

Practical Application

Learning to read is a form of listening for the learner. Young children engage in reading readiness activities such as looking at objects and pictures, placing items in gradients, or sequencing things from left to right. When parents and teachers read to a child, they also provide opportunities for the child to develop listening skills that begin the learning process. Prior to the chronological age of four years, children learn primarily by using their senses: seeing, hearing, touching, tasting, and smelling. They first learn to grasp objects; then they build mental pictures and associate names with the objects. In this way speech, and ultimately reading, become a part of the child's intellectual development.[3]

Children learn by listening to the language of adults and playmates. The learning process is initiated through listening and there are a variety of media that teachers can use to gain the attention of the child. Certainly, picture and short story books are the first resources one considers when teaching the very young (birth to two years).

As the child matures, more complex stories should be selected to further enhance the child's vocabulary and listening skills (to say nothing of the sheer enjoyment a story gives). The use of cassette tapes for music or stories is also valuable. Teachers can see the delight on the face of a child who has just successfully pushed the "play" button and begins to hear the music or story. This success is one of the intrinsic rewards in learning.

While children need to be encouraged in independent ventures, they should not always be left to listen alone. Quality teaching is an interactive process. Therefore, to enjoy a song or a story with "my teacher" is a delightful time for both teacher and child.

The use of video tapes also enhances the learning process because they combine both auditory and visual components. Recently I encountered a two-year-old sitting spellbound in front of the television watching "Winnie the Pooh." The video was approximately ten minutes in length and upon conclusion, the child began to sing and mimic Eeyore. This imitation was evidence of attentive listening. However, teachers need to preview any video to be used with children to make certain it is appropriate for the age level of the child. Such a powerful medium must be used carefully.

The computer is the newest technology available to assist the child in developing listening and thinking skills. Games and graphic challenges are marketed for children of all ages. Teachers are cautioned again to preview and select only those software packages that are developmentally suited for the child's needs and cognitive abilities.

Teachers are the guides, facilitators, and encouragers of the learning process. The purpose of using any of the methodologies listed is to entice and motivate the learner to move into the next phase of the learning process—exploring.

Educational Foundation for Practical Application

Nothing in educational theory exists in isolation from other aspects of development. Many theorists consider listening to be the initiator of the learning process, and it behooves us to examine their theories to determine the listening element within each school of thought.

Figure 3 provides a skeletal view of the major educational theories, a few of the significant contributors to each philosophy, and the core components of each theory. These will be discussed in greater detail in Part II.

Proponents of **humanistic philosophy** hold a central belief that the inner aspirations of the learner are personal to the child and are innately good. In this school of thought, each person is self-directing and evolves toward a unique understanding of life. Learners ascribe their own meaning to educational pursuits and interpret and develop their individual direction toward learning.

Teachers who ascribe to this philosophy would seldom, if ever, require a child to memorize a set of facts (such as the multiplication tables), or a poem, or other pertinent data. Rather, learning experiences that teach these same concepts would be employed. For example, tangible and manipulative objects to teach multiplication concepts would be provided, such as, two apples times two apples equal four apples. Advocates of humanistic philosophy assume that there are basic mental structures into which children take in new information, which results in their constant reconstruction of reality.

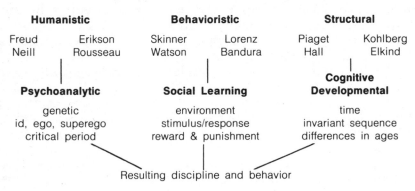

Figure 3
Components of Educational Theories

Humanistic		Behavioristic		Structural	
Freud	Erikson	Skinner	Lorenz	Piaget	Kohlberg
Neill	Rousseau	Watson	Bandura	Hall	Elkind
Psychoanalytic		**Social Learning**		**Cognitive Developmental**	
genetic		environment		time	
id, ego, superego		stimulus/response		invariant sequence	
critical period		reward & punishment		differences in ages	

Resulting discipline and behavior

Humanistic philosophers view the child's intellectual development as that of an organic plant, unique unto itself.[4] The child's personal direction of learning is basically good and should not be interfered with or directed by adults. Children should be allowed, even encouraged, to be creative and spontaneous in their experiences.

In classroom teaching, proponents of humanistic philosophy establish only minimal guidelines and structure for the child's learning environment. There is almost a refusal to impose intellectual and ethical values. They believe it is far superior to capitalize on a child's interest in a particular topic rather than teach something that is foreign to the child's experience or that is at a time deemed inconvenient by the child.

This philosophical approach for the Christian can be difficult to adopt because Scripture outlines in Genesis 1 that people are sinful and fallen creatures, which is diametrically opposed to a belief in the innate goodness of the individual. However, incorporating *some* of the tenets of humanistic philosophy could be appropriate in the Christian education classroom. For example, by respecting the view that learning is enhanced when the child expresses interest in the topic (rather than when the teacher and/or the curriculum decides it is time to teach it), and by allowing the child as much freedom in the classroom as possible, are humanistic elements that might be included in a Christian's personal philosophy for ministry with children.

Educators who hold to **behavioristic philosophy** (see Figure 3) view society and culture as the transmitters of knowledge. These outside influences shape an individual's behavior to make it comply with the will of society. To live as a contributor to society, one needs to conform to the culture's standards of behavior, and this philosophy assumes the culture's extrinsic (external) control in shaping that behavior.

A child's intellect, for behavioristic philosophers, must be molded to conform to culture. It is like a machine—predictable and controllable by someone or something outside of the child.[5] Knowledge is acquired through repetitive actions designed and prescribed by society. Behavior, therefore, is learned and can be ignited or extinguished by an outside source.

In the example of acquiring math facts, a behavioristic teacher typically assigns children a series of problems to solve. For every incorrect response the child receives a negative mark that he or she soon learns to associate with poor grades and dissatisfaction from the teacher. The child begins to make the association between correct responses and teacher satisfaction, thus developing a desire to receive a higher grade and more positive reinforcement from the teacher. Hence the child's learning is reinforced through teacher response and grades.

For the Christian educator, the behavioristic philosophy has merit because if one believes that Scripture teaches that the child is not innately good, it follows that someone is extrinsically needed to shape his or her behavior. There is a story of a child who is told repeatedly by an authority figure to sit down. Finally, the child complies but says, "I'm sitting down on the outside, but I'm still standing on the inside." The child's behavior is shaped by authority figures, but whether it is, in fact, changed is a debatable issue.

Children need moral rules in order to get along and to perpetuate the standards of culture. They depend on adults to provide the input for this. But adults should understand that the child must learn to be self-disciplined rather than be extrinsically controlled into compliant behavior.

Structural philosophers are interested in the intellectual functioning of the individual and the way resultant behavior is explained. They believe that there is an interaction between society and environment that produces a consistent pattern of thinking that does not vary between individuals. They call this an "invariant developmental sequence," which occurs as an intrinsic part of the acquisition of thinking and knowledge. With each new experience, the child adds relevance to what is already known.

Structural philosophers view a child's intellectual development as that of a thinker or philosopher with a changing and progressive ability to reason.[6] The young child reasons differently than adults do and learns to do so through concrete activities. This internal reasoning process is adequate for problem-solving because children develop a progression of ideas, or schema for thinking, that is much the same from individual to individual.

Christian educators should be alert to the fact that "experiencing" or activity-based instruction, and verbal interaction between teacher and child and between child and child are paramount necessities of this educational philosophy. Viewing this approach from a biblical standpoint, that because we are "created in his own image" (Gen. 1:27), it follows that God created the same progression or thinking processes for each individual. These are revealed and adapted in activity and conversation with others that, in turn, promotes intellectual development.

While each of these educational philosophies offers explanations for when and how learning occurs, none of them has adequate scientific evidence to prove its theories to the exclusion of all others. Combining these philosophies in various ways results in different forms of learning theory, which affects the child's resultant behavior and determines or influences methods of discipline used by adults.

Regardless of the educational philosophy employed, teachers know that listening inaugurates and has an impact on the learning process. "Chronologically, children listen before they speak, speak before they read, and read before they write."[7] Listening, as the initiation of learning, is a receptive process and the quality of interpersonal relationships as well as learning depends on one's ability to listen.[8]

> Studies by the Audio Visual Society have shown that among the major skills, listening is way out front as the one we use most each day. The figures show that we listen about 45 percent of our waking hours; we talk about 30 percent of the time; we read around 16 percent of the day; and we write only about 9 percent of the time.[9]

If we spend 45 percent of each day listening, there should be more training available to teach learners how to listen.

Listening can be defined as a "unitary-receptive process [a continuous activity engaged in by the listener] of hearing and selecting, assimilating and organizing, and retaining and covertly responding to aural and nonverbal stimuli."[10] Listening is a communication skill that initiates the learning process. This skill involves both the hearing of sounds and the psychological engagement with the speaker or source of message.[11] In addition to those processes is the

Figure 4
An Outline of Proficient Listening

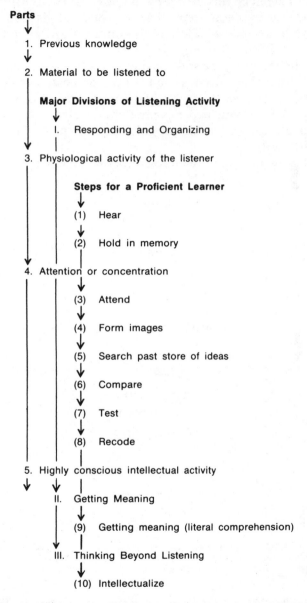

Parts

1. Previous knowledge

2. Material to be listened to

   Major Divisions of Listening Activity

   I.   Responding and Organizing

3. Physiological activity of the listener

   Steps for a Proficient Learner

   (1)   Hear

   (2)   Hold in memory

4. Attention or concentration

   (3)   Attend

   (4)   Form images

   (5)   Search past store of ideas

   (6)   Compare

   (7)   Test

   (8)   Recode

5. Highly conscious intellectual activity

   II.   Getting Meaning

   (9)   Getting meaning (literal comprehension)

   III.   Thinking Beyond Listening

   (10) Intellectualize

Figure 4. Published 1979 by the ERIC Clearinghouse on Reading and Communication Skills and the National Council of Teachers of English. Reprinted with permission. This is Lundsteen, *Listening*, 19.

intellectual activity of the brain at the time of listening and the intellectualizing that occurs after the listening event.[12]

Figure 4 depicts this listening process as it occurs within the learner and outlines ten steps that a proficient listener completes almost simultaneously to allow both communication and reading to occur.[13]

Listening is a complex and continuous series of activities engaged in by the learner that initiates the learning process. The development of language, reading skill, comprehension, clarity of thought, reasoning, and problem-solving depends on a child's ability to listen, but no theory can adequately or thoroughly explain how these processes occur or interrelate.

Figure 5 depicts this listening process as it occurs within the learner.[14]

Figure 5
Listening Model

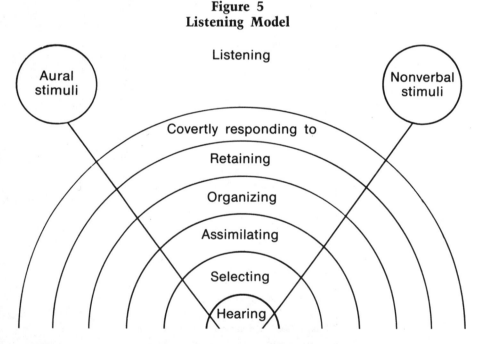

Figure 5. *A Model of the Unitary-Receptive Process of Listening in Oral-Aural Communication.* (Copyright © 1983, reprinted by permission of Holt, Rinehart & Winston) Wolff, et.al. p.8

Without hearing we could not perceive aural stimuli. Without assimilating and organizing the meaning of the aural message, we could not retain data in short-term memory. Nor could we covertly respond to the message and the speaker without retaining data in memory long enough to do so.[15]

The listening process is "unitary" as it happens practically simultaneously with the successful completion of all the other formations listed in Figure 5 for the receiver of information. Theorists have noted the connection that seems to exist between systems of hearing, listening, seeing, perceiving, coupled with psychological involvement and attention and/or concentration on the part of the learner. Researchers in all fields of child development show that listening is essential to the development of reading and reasoning skills.[16]

Truly, as creations of God, we are fearfully and wonderfully made (Psalm 139:14). And as his creatures, we have the most to learn when we listen to him in his Word. As teachers of the Scriptures, we can be encouraged that what we have to share with children opens more doors to them than anything else . . . as they listen.

ENDNOTES

[1]Edgar Dale, *Building a Learning Environment* (Bloomington, Ind.: Phi Delta Kappa, Inc., 1972), 42.

[2]This diagram was used by the International Center for Learning of Gospel Light Publications in teacher training workshops. The visual model was designed by a group of Christian educators. There are other diagrams and explanations for the learning process but the model presented in Figure 2 is one that is developmentally sound, and is teachable to laypersons in the church. It is adapted for use in this text with permission granted by the original publisher.

[3]Rita Watrin and Paul Hanley Furfey, *Learning Activities for the Young Preschool Child* (New York: D. Van Nostrand Co., 1978), 1–5.

[4]Kathleen V. Hoover-Dempsey, 1981, lectures in educational psychology, Peabody College, Nashville, Tenn.

[5]Ibid.

[6]Ibid.

[7]Sara W. Lundsteen, *Listening: Its Impact at All Levels on Reading and the Other Language Arts* (Urbana, Ill.: The National Council of Teachers of English, 1979), 3.

[8]Robert Bolton, *People Skills: How to Assert Yourself, Listen to Others and Resolve Conflicts* (New York: Touchstone Books, 1979), 30.

[9]Robert L. Montgomery, *Listening Made Easy: How to Improve Listening on the Job, at Home, and in the Community* (New York: AMACOM, 1981), 16–17.

[10]Florence I. Wolff et al., *Perceptive Listening* (New York: Holt, Rinehart & Winston, 1983), 8. Copyright © 1983 by Holt, Rinehart and Winston, Inc., reprinted by permission of the publisher.

[11]Ibid.

[12]Ibid., 17, 18.

[13]Lundsteen, *Listening*, 19.

[14]Wolff, et al., *Perceptive Listening*, 8.

[15]Ibid., 9.

[16]John Downing, *Reading and Reasoning* (New York: Springer-Verlag, 1979), 5.

41

ADDITIONAL RESOURCES

Brown, Roger. *A First Language: The Early Stages.* London: Allen and Unwin, 1973.

Cedar, Paul A. *7 Keys to Maximum Communication.* Wheaton, Ill.: Tyndale House, 1980.

Erickson, Kenneth A. *The Power of Communication for Richer Interpersonal Relationships.* St. Louis: Concordia, 1986.

Stott, John R.W. *Your Mind Matters.* Downers Grove, Ill.: InterVarsity Press, 1972.

Vygotsky, Lev S. *Thought and Language.* Cambridge, Mass.: Massachusetts Institute of Technology Press, 1962.

Wilhoit, Jim, and Leland Ryken. *Effective Bible Teaching.* Grand Rapids: Baker, 1988.

Chapter 2

First-Hand Explorers
Learn More

The phases of the learning process are interdependent: the value of each is enhanced by and dependent upon the child's successful accomplishments in the previous phases. The learning process is cyclical (see Figure 6 in this chapter), and no part of the cycle can be omitted if understanding and meaning are to accompany the learning that has taken place. To have enough information to *explore* a concept (the second phase of the learning process), a child must first have *listened* sufficiently to know the variables in the subject under study. For example, if friendship is the topic of study, David and Jonathan are appropriate biblical characters for the child to investigate during the course of study. Listening and recalling their names—David and Jonathan—as the topics/people to be studied, children could ask: Who were they? How did they meet? What happened to cause their friendship to grow? This is the beginning of the exploring phase.

In the traditional classroom, teachers teach (tell) and learners listen for (receive) information and develop concepts. But teachers may have a different view about the way learning takes place. In non-traditional classrooms, teachers allow, encourage, and guide learners into active participation in the learning process.

Learning in an active, participative classroom takes place when a child "digs" for biblical treasures without pressure. The objective is still to learn, but how learning takes place is distinctly different from the way it was in the classrooms of our parents and grandparents. The student is still responsible for the truth to be learned, but the role of the teacher is different. The teacher is the child's facilitator and guide through the process.

Exploring is the second phase of the learning process found in Figure 6.

Figure 6
The Learning Process[1]
(Exploring)

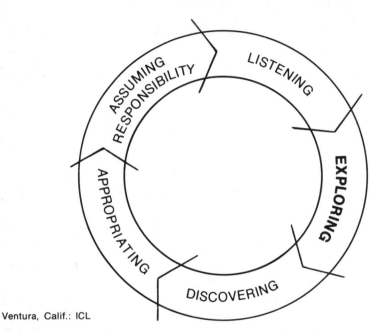

Ventura, Calif.: ICL

EXPLORING

In the learning process, listening to acquire information is a precursor for educational exploration. While knowledge is cumulative and somewhat hierarchical in design and concept, the learner is in charge of what will, in fact, be learned.[2] Learning is intrinsic, that is, it takes place within the child and is his or her activity. The child owns what is learned. Teachers need to realize this and plan their teaching sessions to include a variety of activities that provide first-hand, extrinsic exposure to concepts that can foster and produce the intrinsic learning that the child owns.

Exploring is a *learner-oriented* function in the learning process. This is sometimes a difficult realization for teachers. Autocratic teachers in traditional classrooms are very comfortable controlling information the learner is supposed to acquire. They are frequently less skilled in helping children select those activities that will encourage the acquisition of knowledge and understanding.

Primarily, teachers teach the way they were taught with little regard for what has been discovered about children, learning, and teaching. When the stress and pressure of classroom preparations begin to mount, teachers often revert to reproducing their own learning experiences in the classroom. Teachers need to constantly remind themselves that while they are responsible for almost all that takes place in the classroom, the child controls what will be learned.

Traditional classroom teaching where the teacher is the instructor, the primary focus, and the extrinsic source of information severely limits the learning opportunities provided for children. Teachers who give credence to what has been learned through research in educational psychology appreciate the individual differences evident in every classroom. They provide enrichment activities to the curriculum that encourage children to pursue their interests through a variety of resources. If the child controls what is learned intrinsically, then both instructional experiences and enrichment activities become extrinsic educational opportunities from which the child will draw information and, ultimately, knowledge.

A distinction should be made between instructional and enrichment activities. Parents, a child's first teachers, in their enthusiasm to provide learning experiences for their children, frequently err on the side of instructional pressure to achieve. The father of a five-year-old boy once told me that after dinner every evening, he and his son worked on reciting the American presidents in chronological order. It was obvious that he was awaiting my delighted response for such a venture, and he was disappointed when I queried, "Why would you do this?" I was appalled that people would spend their time learning trivia that would promptly be forgotten by a five-year-old because it didn't relate to anything else the child was learning. This is an example of learning with an instructional emphasis. (See Elkind's books listed in Additional Resources at the end of this chapter for further study about pressuring children to learn.)

Appropriate instructional experiences in the Christian education classroom include having children look up Scripture verses that relate to a theme or to the objective of the day.

Appropriate enrichment activities might include the opportunity to explore some picture books of classical art, to work on one's own picture, or to write creatively. Enrichment activities also include reinforcement projects like drawing a cartoon strip of the Bible story, writing a poem, putting new lyrics to a familiar tune, or filling in the blanks on a student page included in the curriculum.

First-hand exploration of Scripture for whatever is being learned, allows the Holy Spirit to have a profound impact on the learning process.

> To illustrate this point, think about the times you have read the same Scripture over and over, and then some word or phrase that you had never previously noticed leaped off the page at you. At last! A discovery was made through personal, first-hand exploration and involvement with the text. The teacher didn't tell you it was there, but you found it on your own. Frequently this kind of experience leads us into the concordance, Bible dictionary, or commentary to find out more about the passage.

Biblical Principles

Scripture underscores the need for first-hand contact with truth through exploration. In Colossians 1:9–12, Paul tells the people that he is praying for them, but he is also very aware that they hold within them the power to become all that God intended them to be.

Paul wants them to be worthy servants, pleasing God, bearing fruit, and constantly growing in the knowledge of God. Servants need to bear fruit if the church is to grow and prosper. The fruits of the Spirit are outlined in Galatians 5:22–25: "love, joy, peace, patience, kindness, goodness, faithfulness, gentleness and self-control." These are abstract concepts, none of which is acquired by the believer from the teacher. The teacher may model the fruits of the Spirit, but the acquisition of these qualities is controlled by the Holy Spirit in the life of the believer. Learning, doing, being, and becoming all that God intended are accomplished intrinsically, within the student.

Practical Application

The exploration portion of the learning process should be initiated by doing the necessary research on the subject under study. For example, if a teaching unit is planned on the festivals in the Old Testament, the children need to focus on what the Bible reveals about them and on information from other resources in the church library.

The learning that takes place in a unit on the festivals is enhanced when the children look for information and find it themselves, rather than having the teacher tell them all they need to know. They need to become personally involved in studying the topic, issue, or concept. A child who finds the dimensions of the booth in the Feast of Booths through his or her own research can begin to appreciate the problems of constructing a booth. Think of the learning that would take place when the children actually build a booth! The food consumed in festival celebrations can also be researched, prepared, and eaten by the class in order to give them a sensory experience of the food of Bible times. Involvement in the learning process is a motivator for individual learning. When the teacher plans to involve learners, respect for the child, trust in his or her abilities, and encouragement for further learning are communicated.[3] While it is far easier and faster for the teacher to provide children with the necessary information, the results are less lasting.

If all we want is for children to regurgitate data, then acquiring knowledge just by listening to the teacher will suffice. But if the educational goal of our instruction is to develop the critical-thinking skill and confidence in problem solving needed to be a self-disciplined individual then we have no choice but to involve children in exploring resources for learning first-hand. If we want our learners to become competent and capable, we must plan for participative activities in the classroom. This leads a child to a healthy view of self and emphasizes each child's contribution to the learning that is going on in the class. Children need to learn that they can read, comprehend, and contribute significantly to the group. Teachers need to make the resources for learning available to the children and provide some guidelines on how to explore them. The point is that children need to explore the materials themselves and find the pearls of information hidden in the pages of books, maps, and other resources.

Participation in a class study or project makes the classroom into a "microcosm of our culture." If our ultimate desire is that children become productive, contributing members of society, we need to plan ways for them to work cooperatively, be industrious in their discoveries, and share the information with other children. In short, Christian education needs to be experiential. For too long, the church has treated the child as a passive observer in the learning process. Christian education as a discipline needs to respect learners—they can and must be active throughout the learning process.

Some years ago, because our church was considering building a nursery facility, I visited churches of comparable size to discover what others were providing. I was appalled at what I found.

One church was quite anxious to show me its recently renovated nursery rooms. The Director of Christian Education was enthusiastically describing what they had done as we made our way to the area.

When he opened the door to one room, I was stunned. Before me was a large space designed for eighteen-month-old children that contained a huge, low, kidney-shaped table with eighteen small chairs (with seat belts) pulled to its edge. The shape of the table did allow the teacher to reach and touch the children, but the intent was that they not get out of their seats—they must listen to the teacher to learn the lesson of the day. Except perhaps for instructional methodology, no thought had been given to the physical, social, emotional, intellectual, or spiritual needs of the toddlers who occupied that room. There were no books, no play equipment, and no artwork displayed on the walls. And this church had a reputation for providing quality children's programming! All these children could do was to listen to the lesson the teacher had prepared. No consideration had been given to how children learn nor to what activities might enrich the learning process. As learners, these children received little respect.

If exploring is a significant phase in the learning process, then we must create opportunities for exploration projects and use methods appropriate for the age of the child. "Children find meaning through discovery (perhaps even by chance), exploration, investigation, and participation."[4] To provide opportunities for children to explore biblical truth for themselves requires patience, planning, and perseverance, on the part of the teacher. The Bible should be a handy resource for children; becoming familiar with its contents is critical to their ultimate spiritual development.

Allowing first grade children to look up Bible verses for themselves is taxing, but they can do it—and they *want* to do it, given enough time and encouragement. The table of contents should be used to acquaint the children with the order of the books of the Bible. Even beginning readers can find the book of John in the New Testament and can locate the big number for chapter 12 and the smaller numbers for the verses, 5 and 6. But teachers need to be patient, help only when absolutely necessary, and then sit back and appreciate the sounds of their students' voices as they begin to read more and more of each passage. Obviously, they will need assistance with some of the words when they begin, but by the end of the first grade, most of the children will be able to read a large percentage of the words in each verse. Teachers should persevere in having children get into God's Word. Such a note of pride comes into their voices when they finish the reading and they look to the teacher for acknowledgment for the job they have done!

> Teachers, we must not deny children these opportunities for success in exploring God's Word first-hand!

There is a difference between teachers who tell their learners everything and those who allow their learners to explore and discover it for themselves. Which kind of teacher are you? Teachers who only lecture learners think they are teaching more; however, respecting the abilities of the learner to explore biblical truth personally will allow the learner to retain more and to retain it longer. "Teach less but teach it more thoroughly" is a common theme in Madeline Hunter's workshops, and this should become the battle cry for teachers. Teachers need to devise ways to make learning a joy through involvement rather than make it an auditory drudgery.

The facts of Scripture are readily available. "But despite all the biblical information available, the church is often lacking in maturity and spiritual understanding, and its biblical illiteracy is often alarming."[5] What teachers need to focus on in the classroom is training children as believers who know, understand, and apply the biblical truth they learn.

In a kindergarten class, the children were studying a unit on being kind to neighbors. The children had listened to what God's Word said on the topic and had even experienced a learning activity to reinforce the concept. But when the children were dismissed, one young man walked out into the hall and promptly proceeded to slug the first child in his path. He may have given assent to learning in the class, but he did not follow through in changing his behavior in accordance with what he had been taught! Knowing, understanding, and applying biblical truth necessitates completing all the phases of the learning process. Teachers are teaching material that is life-changing, so they need to do it in such a way as to excite their learners to explore God's Word *first-hand*.

Educational Foundation for Practical Application

Frequently, Christian educators believe their only responsibility is to concentrate on the spiritual aspect of child development. Scripture, however, outlines a more wholistic approach and, therefore, educators need to examine the broad spectrum of educational philosophies and learning theories.

In Deuteronomy 6:5, the writer states that one should

Love the LORD your God with all your heart [emotional development] and with all your soul [spiritual development] and with all your strength [physical development].

The New Testament records a more complete developmental picture in the words of Jesus:

"Love the Lord your God with all your heart [emotional development], and with all your soul [spiritual development], and with all your strength [physical development] and with all your mind [intellectual development]; and, 'Love your neighbor as yourself [social development].' " (Luke 10:27)

God created us with minds and he intends us to use them in relationship to other people. He desires that Christian educators help children develop wholistically. All educational philosophies and learning theories must be examined, therefore, to discern their views on humanity; then applications can be made for the Christian education classroom.

Christian educators need to study the various educational philosophies because, with Scripture, they shape our views of the educational goals and methods that form our world and life view. "The philosophy of education is the attempt to bring the insights and methods of philosophy to bear on the educational enterprise,"[6] writes Michael L. Peterson. Christian educators need to be aware of these philosophies (see Chapter 1) and consider how each of them approaches the pragmatic issues that shape classroom practice.

Educators who adhere to **humanistic philosophy** (See Figure 3, p. 34) generally view learning in psychoanalytic terms. According to Peterson's (1986) summary of the philosophical issues outlined in his book, *Philosophy of Education: Issues and Options*, these educators would likely be comfortable with the idealists and existentialists.[7] Learning theorists adopting these presuppositions view the child as basically good and hold that knowledge develops from immediate, inner experiences and aspirations of the self.

A teacher who views the child as innately good and capable of self-direction will provide few limits and boundaries for exploration. Freedom becomes a prerequisite for learning to think, to feel, and to develop personal values—all issues that produce human beings of eminent worth.

Psychoanalytic/humanistic learning theorists discuss the issues of heredity and environment, or the nature-nurture debate, and their effects on human development. Hereditarians view human characteristics as transmitted through genes from previous generations. Henry E. Goddard, G. Stanley Hall, Lewis Terman, and Arnold Gesell were proponents of this theory.

Environmentalists argue that children are shaped by the nurturing opportunities within their surroundings. John Locke, John B. Watson, and B. F. Skinner were adherents to this view.[8] This faction gave rise to the behavioristic philosophy of education.

The historic debate between hereditarians and environmentalists can never be resolved because educational psychologists have since researched these variables and have learned that each has an impact on the other in child development. The humanistic psychologist sees children as the controllers of their own learning, thus they should be self-directed in their educational pursuits. This self-direction allows children to investigate topics of their own choosing, allowing them to evolve in their own unique ways.[9]

Educators who embrace **behavioristic philosophy** are most likely social-learning theorists. Naturalists (using Peterson's philosophical terminology) are probably also included in this category. Behaviorists want to study human behavior without regard for inner motivations. These behaviorists, among whom B. F. Skinner reigns supreme, believed that children could be trained to behave in much the same way as rats and pigeons are. However, Jerome Bruner, another contributor to this learning theory, believed that learning could not be explained without observing children in the classroom. Most likely, a combination of these two approaches within the behavioristic philosophical context is responsible for the development and acceptance of behavior modification in American school classrooms.

Skinner reduced the educational process to two basic functions: operant conditioning and conditioned reinforcement. In his research, he found that environmental stimuli produced a response. In operant conditioning, the response occurs spontaneously, followed immediately by conditioned reinforcement.

This principle can best be illustrated by describing a product and a process for toilet training developed by Skinner. The product was an infant toilet seat equipped with a music box. The process involved the reward of music being played when the weight of the child's urine in the container was sufficient enough to activate the music box.[10] The operant conditioning in this example of voluntary behavior is the child's ability to urinate in the container. The conditioned reinforcement of this stimuli is the music that played immediately upon receipt of the necessary weight of the urine.

Bruner would likely applaud this approach to toilet training because it involves children as the primary controllers of their environment. He believed they could be taught practically anything, but that their instruction should not be limited to the mere facts of a subject. He stressed the intuition involved in the problem-solving steps in analysis.[11]

Educators who adopt a **structuralist** view of child development will likely approach learning theory from a cognitive-development standpoint. Peterson's description of Neo-Thomists and experimentalists shows their consistency with this approach to learning.[12] John Dewey and Jean Piaget are contributors to this view of development. Cognitive-developmentalists look at learning in terms of a child's active and natural interaction with the environment and the ordered pattern of thinking in problem-solving that results.

Dewey believed an experienced-based curriculum would accomplish two goals: more effective learning and greater competence in living.[13] Dewey is credited with having tremendous influence on modern education because he envisioned a child-centered curriculum that would involve children in the process of learning. Yet some Christian educators (particularly evangelicals) have disparaged the movement from a content-based curriculum to a child-centered orientation of activity, interaction, interest, and creativity. I applaud the stance taken by Gangel and Benson on this subject:

> The intelligent approach to Dewey then, it would seem, would have to be one that excludes his godless philosophy and adapts his practical methodology. . . . If the excesses can be avoided, Christian education can make valid use of Dewey's principles in the learning process.[14]

Christian educators must be knowledgeable about both Scripture and educational theories, so that they can make well-informed decisions about how to put theories into practice.

Piaget is famous for having identified, through his observations of and interviews with children, a series of sequential and invariant stages of intellectual development. Piaget states that "intelligence is, by definition, adaptation to new situations, so there is a continual construction of structures."[15] While the term "stage" implies a clearly defined criteria for movement, educators who know children are aware that even though the stages are associated with specific chronological ages, the movement from one stage to the next is gradual, and not easily recognizable at the appointed yearly age. But older children do think differently than their younger counterparts. Figure 7 is derived from Piaget's work on cognitive theory.

Figure 7
Sequence of Cognitive Structures[16]
Sensorimotor Period — birth to two years

Stage 1: birth to one month
    a. highly visually skilled
    b. automatic sucking reflex

Stage 2: one to four months
    a. primary circular motions of thumb to mouth
    b. receives cues for sucking—same position to be fed, then sucking, then satisfaction of need
    c. develops curiosity of surroundings
    d. imitates successful acts

Stage 3: four to ten months
    a. secondary circular motions of crawling and manipulating things
    b. accidentally grasps toys

Stage 4: ten to twelve months
    a. anticipates action which previously happened accidentally
    b. coordinates secondary schema when the primary goal attainment was denied

Stage 5: twelve to eighteen months
    a. begins to walk
    b. searches for novelty

Stage 6: eighteen months to two years
    a. beginning of thought

Preconceptual Period — two to four years

1. egocentric—does not understand another's perspective
2. classifies objects by a single characteristic

Intuitive Period — four to seven years

1. remains egocentric
2. begins to classify things into groups
3. uses numbers but cannot explain why
4. imitates models
5. requires explanation to achieve understanding

Concrete Operational Period — seven to eleven years

1. focuses on several aspects of a situation simultaneously
2. can reverse the direction of thought
3. sensitive to transformation of thought
4. may display different levels of achievement in operations requiring similar processes

Formal Operational Period — eleven years and above

1. mental operations reach a high degree of equilibrium (thought is flexible and effective)
2. deals efficiently with complex problems of reasoning
3. imagines many possibilities inherent in a situation
4. thoughts transcend the here and now

A thorough study of these ages and stages reveals that children under eleven years of age have difficulty understanding abstract concepts. Granted, they may parrot adults' words and expressions, but real understanding will come later in their cognitive developmental processes. Again, be reminded that although there are specific ages associated with each stage, these ages must be applied with latitude. If Christian educators want children to know and understand abstract concepts, they must make those concepts concrete for the child.

For example, during a missions conference with an emphasis on Christlikeness, our learning objective for the children was that they understand that Jesus is our model and that he provides the pattern for living. Because our group ranged in age from six to thirteen and because we believe that Piaget is correct as to when a child can comprehend abstract concepts, we struggled to determine how to make the concept of Christlikeness concrete.

Our method of accomplishing this was to give every child some fabric and a piece of a dress pattern. Each child cut out his or her piece of material according to the pattern piece in preparation for assembling the entire garment. We used the fabric as illustrative of our individual selves, without shape or purpose on our own. Using the "pattern" of Christ's life, we "cut out" our lives to be like his (Christlike). We become functional and purposeful and important pieces of his "whole garment" when fitted together as the body of Christ.

Christian educators do not have to know all the details of educational philosophy and learning theory, but they need to know enough about the key concepts to determine which elements are consistent with Scripture. Christian educators should examine curriculum and teaching practices carefully. Some issues, topics, and concepts are frequently taught inappropriately to very young children with undeveloped cognitive abilities. That is not to say that these abstract concepts should not be taught. Rather educators must devise appropriate intellectual approaches that help children understand the realities of the Christian life.

ENDNOTES

[1]Adapted from International Center For Learning (Ventura, Calif.: Gospel Light Publications). Used by permission of the publisher.

[2]Earline Kendall and Mary Ellen Drushal, "A Climate for Classroom Management," *Everybody's Business: A Book About School Discipline*, (Columbiaa, S.C.: Southeastern Public Education Program), 1980.

[3]Don Dinkmeyer and Rudolf Dreikurs, *Encouraging Children to Learn: The Encouragement Process* (Englewood Cliffs, N.J.: Prentice-Hall, 1963).

[4]Dorothy Jean Furnish, *Exploring the Bible with Children* (Nashville: Abingdon, 1975), 16.

[5]Jim Wilhoit and Leland Ryken, *Effective Bible Teaching* (Grand Rapids: Baker, 1988), 28.

[6]Michael L. Peterson, *Philosophy of Education: Issues and Options* (Downers Grove, Ill.: InterVarsity Press, 1986), 17. All references to this text are used by permission of InterVarsity Press, P.O. Box 1400, Downers Grove, Ill. 60515.

[7]Ibid.

[8]Richard C. Sprinthall and Norman A. Sprinthall, *Educational Psychology: A Developmental Approach*, 3d ed. (New York: Random House, 1981).

[9]Lee J. Cronbach, *Educational Psychology*, 3d ed. (New York: Harcourt Brace Jovanovich, Inc., 1977).

[10]Sprinthall & Sprinthall, *Educational Psychology*.

[11]Ibid.

[12]Peterson, *Philosophy of Education*.

[13]Sprinthall & Sprinthall, *Educational Psychology*.

[14]Kenneth O. Gangel and Warren S. Benson, *Christian Education: Its History & Philosophy* (Chicago: Moody Press, 1983), 303–4.

[15]Jean-Claude Bringuier, *Conversations with Jean Piaget* (Chicago and London: Univ. of Chicago Press, 1980), 42.

[16]Herbert Ginsburg and Sylvia Opper, *Piaget's Theory of Intellectual Development: An Introduction* (Englewood Cliffs, N.J.: Prentice-Hall, 1969). Adapted by permission of Prentice Hall, Inc., Englewood Cliffs, N.J.

ADDITIONAL RESOURCES

Blankenbaker, Frances, ed. *What the Bible Is All About For Young Explorers.* Ventura, Calif.: Regal, 1986.

Bruner, Jerome S. *The Process of Education.* New York: Vintage, 1960.

Cremin, Lawrence A. *Traditions of American Education.* New York: Basic, Inc., 1977.

Cully, Iris V., and Kendig Brubaker Cully, eds. *Process and Relationship: Issues in Theology, Philosophy and Religious Education.* Birmingham, Ala.: Religious Education Press, 1978.

Elkind, David. *All Grown Up & No Place to Go: Teenagers in Crisis.* Reading, Mass.: Addison-Wesley, 1984.

————. *The Child and Society: Essays in Applied Child Development.* New York: Oxford Univ. Press, 1979.

————. *The Hurried Child.* Reading, Mass.: Addison-Wesley, 1981.

————. *Miseducation: Preschoolers at Risk.* New York: Alfred A. Knopf, 1987.

Joy, Donald M. *Meaningful Learning in the Church.* Winona Lake, Ind.: Light and Life, 1969.

Knight, George R. *Philosophy & Education: An Introduction in Christian Perspective.* Berrien Springs, Mich.: Andrews Univ, Press, 1980.

Kolb, David A. *Experiential Learning: Experience as the Source of Learning and Development.* Englewood Cliffs, N.J.: Prentice-Hall, 1984.

Lee, James Michael. *The Flow of Religious Instruction: A Social Science Approach.* Birmingham, Ala.: Religious Education Press, 1973.

Pazmino, Robert W. *Foundational Issues in Christian Education: An Introduction in Evangelical Perspective.* Grand Rapids: Baker, 1988.

Piaget, Jean. *The Moral Judgment of the Child.* New York: The Free Press, 1965.

————. *Play, Dreams and Imitation in Childhood.* New York: W. W. Norton, 1962.

Skinner, B. F. *Science and Human Behavior.* New York: The Free Press, 1953.

Taylor, Marvin J., ed. *Foundations for Christian Education in an Era of Change.* Nashville: Abingdon, 1976.

Chapter 3

"Seek and Ye Shall Find"

One of the joys of childhood is **discovery**. An infant discovers that there are toes on the end of his feet and that they are delightful to chew. A slightly older child sees the paraphernalia in the kitchen and is driven by curiosity to explore *all* of those things—much to the dismay of her parents! There are pan lids to be banged, dog food to be tasted, and magazines to be shredded. No adult has told the infant that these things are there to be done. The child instinctively desires to explore and discover.

Mountain climbers scale Mt. Everest for the same reason: because it is there!

Learning is much the same. Children learn because they are curious about things in their environment; they are intrinsically motivated to investigate. Children who are deprived of opportunities for independent discovery will likely become discouraged and begin to doubt their abilities to accomplish anything. This results in stunted development on all levels.

Discovering is the third phase of the learning process found in Figure 8.

DISCOVERING

In participative/experiential learning, the discovering phase of the learning process is where the real enjoyment of learning takes place. Listening and exploring are work, but discovery is fun. Children are guided by teachers in the process of discovering, but the age-level appropriateness and the meaningfulness of the activity must be right for the real joy of learning to come.

Figure 8
The Learning Process[1]
(Discovering)

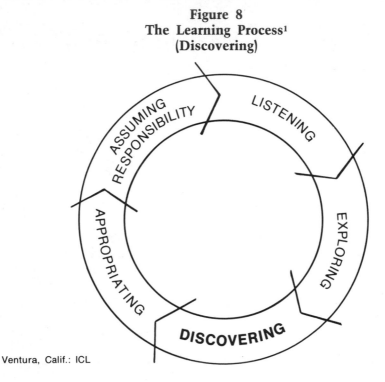

Ventura, Calif.: ICL

The "Eureka" experiences in learning almost always come through personal exploration and discovery. "In a child-centered approach [to learning], the ultimate value of a particular learning activity lies in the quality of the experience as such as it relates directly to the felt needs and personal satisfaction of the learner."[2] James Michael Lee outlines ten key findings about learning in his book, *The Flow of Religious Instruction: A Social Science Approach.* Among those key findings is the meaningfulness of the learning experience itself. "Thus a direct, immediate, firsthand experience tends to produce more effective learning than one which is indirect, mediate, or vicarious."[3]

This reminds the Christian educator that discovery occurs through firsthand experience in activities that are age-level appropriate and meaningful to the experiences of the child. Having fifth grade children construct bird feeders out of pine cones, peanut butter, and bird seed is not an age-level appropriate activity, nor is it likely to provide a meaningful experience for ten-year-olds. Kindergarten children are more likely to appreciate and enjoy this type of activity.

Biblical Principles

In 2 Corinthians 12, Paul mentions his "thorn in the flesh" that he desired God to remove. But instead of taking the "thorn" away, God reminded Paul, "My grace is sufficient for you, for my power is made perfect in weakness" (v. 9). Paul had to experience the reality of a thorn in the flesh so that he could discover the source of his true strength.

In a letter to the Ephesians, Paul wrote, "I pray also that the eyes of your heart may be enlightened in order that you may know the hope to which he has called you, the riches of his glorious inheritance in the saints. . . . " (Eph. 1:18–19). This was a prayer that God would give them personal understanding. But it could only come to them as they discovered truth for themselves.

To write meaningfully on tablets of human hearts, Christian educators need to allow children to discover biblical truth for themselves, because herein lies the long-term power for committed servanthood. If children observe but never experience the delight of Scripture, they are much more likely to grow up to become spectators in the church. If we let them personally explore and discover the truth contained in Scripture, then it becomes a personal discovery they can appropriate to the fullest.

Practical Application

The educational foundation for activity-based curriculum was laid in the previous chapter. The question now is: How do children learn?

> Perhaps the term learning defies definition because learning, although it occurs in all of us, is complex and involves many variables, such as maturation, readiness, atmosphere, motivation, and a host of other factors. . . . Learning has to do with developing for functioning. It affects the whole person and cannot be separated from human experience and behavior. It involves the acquisition of information, data, and knowledge, as well as changes in behavior."[4]

The third phase of the learning process (discovering) is so closely aligned with the second phase of exploring that it is difficult to discern when one phase ends and the other begins. No definitive line of demarcation between the two can be drawn.

Figure 9
Dale's Cone of Learning[5]

EDGAR DALE
Professor of Education
Ohio State University

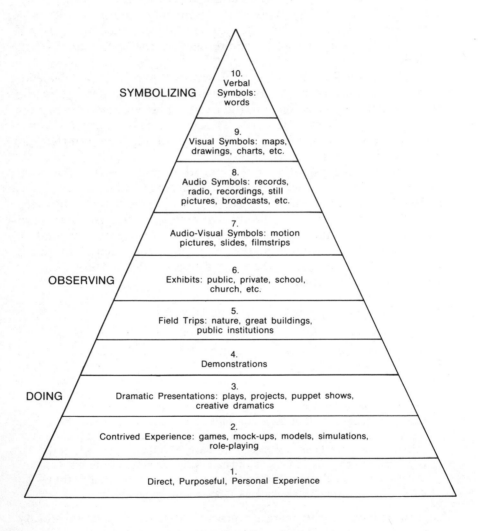

Over the years, educational researchers have found that direct experience, which elicits personal discovery, is the learning that is retained longest. In Figure 9, Edgar Dale synthesizes relevant educational research into a "Cone of Learning," that depicts the degree of effectiveness of each teaching method.

This cone illustrates the rate of retention—long term learning—when combined with various methods of instruction, from abstract and impersonal means at the peak to concrete, personal experiences at the base. Learning can take place at any point in the cone. In fact, quality teaching will use all methods. But if we desire children to learn for a lifetime, we need to concentrate on the activities that allow their participation. Involvement sets the stage for discovery.

In a preschool classroom of learners studying Mary, Joseph, and Jesus' flight to Egypt (Matt. 2:13–23), the learning objective might be for the children to know that God cares and provides for children. The teacher might provide some suitcases to pack and some dress-up clothes for the journey so that the children can role-play the event. By asking such questions as, "Would you like to travel a great distance on a donkey?" or "What do you take with you when you go on a long trip?" the teacher can help the child discover some of the difficulties experienced by Jesus' family as they made this journey.

School-age children studying the same Bible story will be able to do some map study to determine the distance from Bethlehem to Egypt, and estimate how long it would take to travel that route by donkey. Some learners might like to make a mural depicting some of the scenes along the way to Egypt or draw a cartoon strip about the journey. If children are to learn more than the facts of the story, we must allow them—encourage them—to use their vivid imaginations to discover some of the things that might have been encountered on this trip.

Children need the freedom to explore. In our American heritage, freedom is usually thought to be freedom from restraints or confinements in any form. That is not the kind of freedom needed in the Christian education classroom. Neither is it the freedom of A. S. Neill's Summerhill Farm, where children did what they wanted when they desired. But freedom to explore within predetermined parameters is another way of respecting the abilities and genius of being a child.

Once our church's educational ministry designed a vacation Bible school program using "The Marketplace in Jesus' Day," an Augsburg Press idea we adapted to our needs. We displayed samples of the sandals, carpenter tools, a fisherman's net, an oil lamp, and bread that was likely to have been a part of Jesus' life so that the children could see, feel, and smell what life was like in Bible times. But this format did not permit or accommodate their personal creative expression and children need opportunities to explore through creative expression. Therefore the format for our VBS was an open classroom where children were free to move from center to center as they desired. We had several centers filled with information the children needed in order to appreciate the period when Jesus walked on this earth. There were also centers where the children could actually make leather sandals, or a carpenter tool of the day, or a fishermen's net, or an oil lamp, or make and eat unleavened bread, or write a Bible verse in Greek letters, etc.

During our evaluation session at the close of the first day, we discovered that many children were thoroughly enjoying the results of their work in the discovery centers, but had conveniently avoided the content/input centers. Therefore, on the second day, their freedom to participate in the marketplace centers was dependent upon their earning three different colored chips that could be acquired only in the content/input centers.

In that way we knew they had listened and explored biblical content. Their freedom to explore required some minimal limitations to assure that they were getting the information they needed to understand what they were experiencing. They needed content before they could truly experience the joy of discovering what it was like to make and use the various products featured in the marketplace shops.

Curricula in school and in Sunday school generally provide multiple opportunities for cognitive growth and development, but seldom does the curriculum (or teachers for that matter) give attention to the child's affective area of life. Appreciation of music, drama, storytelling, and dance comes through involvement in those activities.

Take the earlier example of Mary, Joseph, and Jesus traveling to Egypt by donkey. The classical composition of Ferde Grofe's *Grand Canyon Suite* has a theme called "On the Trail," which evokes the steady clip-clop and whinny of the pack animals. The children could experience the music and express their responses through paint or clay. They could move in rhythm to the music as they imagine what it might be like to travel by donkey.

Providing opportunities for children to be creative, urges them toward self-discovery of their God-given abilities and talents. When teaching in a classroom, I seldom display samples of whatever art project is scheduled for the day. Then every child's product is unique and an expression of the inner self. When a sample is provided, the children usually copy it and make it as nearly like the teacher's as possible. Creativity requires innovation. It requires reaching into one's deepest soul to discover the gifts waiting there to be explored without reservation or concern for the "acceptability" of the effort. Henri Nouwen writes:

> A gift only becomes a gift when it is received; and nothing we have to give—wealth, talents, competence, or just beauty—will ever be recognized as true gifts until someone opens his [her] hands or heart to accept them.[6]

Teachers can encourage discovery and creativity within children by accepting, acknowledging, respecting, and celebrating each child's effort and gift. Sometimes children need to be supported before they can be sufficiently courageous or confident to create. Unless children can explore the affective domain of learning, they will not be able to discover their ultimate potential in becoming servants of the King. "With the goodness of God to desire our highest welfare, the wisdom of God to plan it, and the power of God to achieve it, what do we lack? Surely we are the most favored of all creatures."[7]

Children need some predetermined structure and order, but within those limits they should be free to discover.

Educational Foundation for Practical Application

When we think about discovery in the learning process, we assume there is involvement on the part of the learner, and that teachers are providing opportunities for learners' participation in Bible study through activities.

A caution should be sounded for teachers at this juncture: the Bible study and activities provided should be age-level appropriate. What does that mean? Study and activities should be offered so that children can be expected to succeed physically and intellectually in the learning goal of the session.

For example, six-year-old children are not likely to comprehend the complexities of the relationship among the persons of the Trinity nor intelligently discuss their views on abortion. They would be incapable of making a significant contribution to activities that focus around those topics. Conversely, for a six-year-old to study about the boy Jesus in the Temple (Luke 2:41–52) would be very simple, because they could relate to Jesus as a child and understand the events outlined in the story.

The age-level appropriateness of study topics and activities is based upon Piagetian findings outlined in Chapter 2, Figure 7 of this text. Why subject children to study and activities that they are unable to comprehend? A sense of inadequacy and inability are likely results in children forced into activities beyond their capabilities. Nothing is more discouraging for children than assignments they are incapable of completing.

When discovery in learning is the desired end, the Christian educator must be cognizant of the needs of the child in all developmental areas—social, emotional, physical, intellectual, and spiritual. To ask a two-year-old to willingly share crayons with another child is akin to requesting him or her to walk a tightrope across Niagara Falls! It is a virtual impossibility. "Mine," is the likely response you will get from such a ridiculous adult request.

Adults can and usually do force the issue and make the child share the crayons, but inwardly, the two-year-old does not understand why this action must be taken and frequently will come forth with loud protests! What a simple thing it would be to provide a box of crayons for every child so that sharing among "two's" did not have to be forced. As Christian educators, let us respect the developing child sufficiently enough to allow each to enter into what adults consider socially appropriate behavior when they are ready.

Another consideration for the classroom is the various styles of learning evidenced among a group. If as Christian educators we are concerned not only with the long-term retention of concepts but also with teaching in the most effective and efficient manner, we must gear our teaching method toward the learning needs of our students. Learning styles are not innate nor constant, but develop with many contributing factors, i.e., personality type or disposition, academic training, career choice, current job or tasks.[8] We want children to learn with as much ease and comfort as possible, since this will encourage them to greater accomplishments and pursuits. We can assist them in this process when we understand how they perceive and process new information.

Through extensive research, David Kolb found that people characteristically choose between abstract and concrete approaches to new information. They process this information either through active or reflective orientation. These two choices between the two dimensions place a learner in one of four learning styles: diverger, assimilator, converger, or accommodator.[9]

Each of these learning styles has a comfort zone associated with the learning that takes place. Teachers typically teach from their own learning style unless they make a conscious effort to provide experiences that incorporate the learning needs of all styles.[10] Christian educators must be aware of the various learning needs present in each child and teach accordingly. (Teaching methods that should be used for learners in each quadrant will be discussed in Part II,

Chapter 7.) Suffice it to say for now that some learners (divergers) need to experience, some (assimilators) require reflection, others (convergers) must conceptualize, and some (accommodators) will experiment with new information and processes they encounter in the learning environment.[11]

ENDNOTES

[1]Adapted from International Center for Learning (Ventura, Calif.: Gospel Light Publications). Used by permission of the publisher.

[2]Willliam C. Nutting, *Designing Classroom Spontaneity: Case-Action Learning* (Englewood Cliffs, N.J.: Prentice-Hall, 1973), ii.

[3]James Michael Lee, *The Flow of Religious Instruction: A Social Science Approach* (Birmingham, Ala.: Religious Press, 1973), 74.

[4]Doris A. Freese, "How Children Think and Learn" in *Childhood Education in the Church: Revised and Expanded*, eds. Robert E. Clark, Joanne Brubaker, and Roy B. Zuck (Chicago: Moody Press, 1986), 68.

[5]Edgar Dale, *Audio-Visual Methods in Teaching*, rev. ed. (New York: Holt, Rinehart and Winston, 1954), 42–56. Diagram from *Audio-Visual Methods in Teaching, Third Edition* by Edgar Dale, copyright © 1969 by Holt, Rinehart and Winston, Inc., reprinted by permission of the publisher.

[6]Henri J. M. Nouwen, *Creative Ministry* (Garden City, N.Y.: Image/Doubleday, 1971), 17.

[7]A. W. Tozer, *The Knowledge of the Holy* (New York: Harper & Row, 1961), 70.

[8]Donna M. Smith and David A. Kolb, *User's Guide for The Learning Style Inventory* (Boston: McBer, 1986).

[9]Ibid.

[10]Claudia E. Cornett, *What You Should Know About Teaching and Learning Styles* (Bloomington, Ind.: Phi Delta Kappa Educational Foundation, 1983).

[11]Bernice McCarthy, *The 4MAT System: Teaching to Learning Styles with Right/Left Mode Techniques* (Barrington, Ill.: EXCEL, 1980).

ADDITIONAL RESOURCES

Bellah, Robert N., Richard Madsen, William M. Sullivan, Ann Swidler, and Steven M. Tipton. *Habits of the Heart: Individualism and Commitment in American Life.* San Francisco: Harper & Row, 1985.

Bennett, Neville, et al. *Teaching Styles and Pupil Progress.* Cambridge, Mass.: Harvard University Press, 1976.

Davidman, Leonard. "Learning Style: The Myth, The Panacea, The Wisdom." *Phi Delta Kappan* (May 1981), 641–45.

Elbow, Peter. *Embracing Contraries: Explorations in Learning and Teaching.* New York: Oxford University Press, 1986.

Fischer, Barbara Bree, and Louis Fischer. "Styles in Teaching and Learning." *Educational Leadership* (January, 1979).

Glasser, Robert. "Education and Thinking: The Role of Knowledge." *American Psychologist,* 39, no. 2 (February, 1984): 93–104.

Messick, Samuel and Assoc. *Individuality in Learning.* San Francisco: Jossey-Bass, 1976.

Miller, C. Dean, Margaret Alway, and Donna L. McKinley. "Effects of Learning Styles and Strategies on Academic Success." *Journal of College Student Personnel,* 28, no. 5 (1987): 399–404.

Chapter 4

Internalizing Truth

"All too often we are giving our young people cut flowers when we should be teaching them to grow their own plants. . . . We think of the mind as a storehouse to be filled when we should be thinking of it as an instrument to be used."[1] This idea is similar to a phrase used by concerned church leaders: "We are training laypersons to be keepers of the aquarium rather than fishers of men!" The church is reaping the seeds of mediocrity and low expectations that it has sown for generations. It has been training people to be spectators and passive observers rather than active participants in learning and in ministry. We have allowed learners to depend on their teachers and have not planned for them to use their minds responsibly.

Sunday school attendance has been declining numerically for decades. Perhaps the church's inability to encourage and allow people to think for themselves is a contributing factor to this decline. This mind-set among Christian educators needs to change if we intend learners to retain information and become inspired for long-term service. Learners need to internalize the truth of Scripture if we expect results from our instruction.

The fourth component in the learning process is **appropriating**. Webster defines appropriating as "to take possession of or make use of exclusively for oneself, often without permission." This definition underscores the belief that the learner controls what is to be learned and is self-selective of all that is offered.

In Figure 10, we see the continual progression of the learning process as the learner arrives at the appropriating phase.

Figure 10
The Learning Process[2]
(Appropriating)

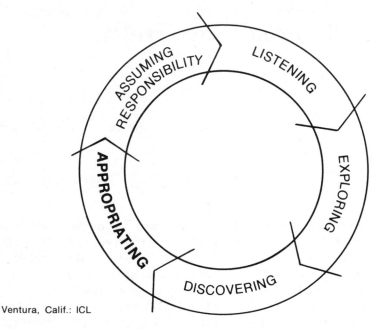

Ventura, Calif.: ICL

This component of the learning process is terribly important because it signals the onset of reflective internalization of what is to be learned. While it is listed as a separate element, it may be occurring simultaneously with the preceeding phase of the learning process.

APPROPRIATING

Appropriating biblical truth takes place as the individual discovers that the content of Scripture is personal and applies to life. For example, the realization that the passage in Malachi 3:10, which tells the believer that the whole tithe is to be brought into the storehouse, is often a startling discovery for children (and some adults too!). The teacher may tell learners that this means bringing ten percent of their earnings to contribute to the church coffers.

They listen to that idea and perhaps explore other Scripture that supports the tithe and then discover how much the whole tithe is by cutting an apple into ten pieces—giving them a tangible, concrete, and visual example. Children look at that tenth piece and see how insignificant it is in comparison to the other nine pieces. Then the Holy Spirit applies the truth that we need to return the tithe to God. The learner discovers that this passage is a personal responsibility and not meant for a friend across the street, on the next farm, or just for adults. The learner needs to say and feel, "This Scripture is talking to me!"

Understanding the relationship between bringing the tithe to the church as an act of love and obedience is probably too abstract for young children to comprehend.[3] Piaget reminds educators that children younger than eleven years have difficulty understanding abstract concepts and therefore they can hardly see the connection between loving obedience and bringing the tithe into the storehouse. How internalization actually takes place in the learning process is a mystery and, like faith, is difficult to describe.

Biblical Principles

The writings of Paul contain many references where learners are reminded that biblical truth is to be applied by them in their daily walks and adhered to throughout their life journeys. In 1 Thessalonians 2:10–12 we read:

> You are witnesses, and so is God, of how holy, righteous and blameless we were among you who believed. For you know that we dealt with each of you as a father deals with his own children, encouraging, comforting and urging you to live lives worthy of God, who calls you into his kingdom and glory.

"To live lives worthy of God" is a life-long process and therefore biblical truth becomes the guide for all of life.

Ephesians 5:1–2 states: "Be imitators of God, therefore, as dearly loved children and live a life of love, just as Christ loved us and gave himself up for us. . . ." Children need to reflect on the fact that the believer's purpose and goal on earth is to know God, to pursue an intimate relationship with him and to serve him forever. This then becomes a primary goal of our instruction.

Practical Application

One of the key issues in appropriating biblical truth is the need for time to internalize the concept being learned. Why are Sunday school teachers always in such a rush to get through the lesson or complete a project already underway? Is it because they know the bell will soon ring, signaling the end of the class period? (Of course, all *good* little boys and girls get done before the bell!) Are Sunday school teachers guilty of pushing and prodding their learners to finish because of the "tyranny of the urgent" without taking time to reflect on important issues? Appropriating takes time and cannot be rushed.

Shawna, a third grader, was completing her illustration of the good Samaritan when her face suddenly took on a reflective look. She asked her teacher, "Does this story mean that I am supposed to help Judy with her math? She always comes to school dirty and wearing a torn dress and nobody wants to be with her." "Yes, Shawna," the teacher replied. "If you are going to be the kind of neighbor Jesus wants you to be, you need to care for those who are less fortunate than you are." Shawna considered what her teacher said, then responded, "I don't want to but I guess nobody in my class wants to either, so I'll be a good Samaritan."

Most of the time the objective of the lesson is not appropriated in the time span of one class session as it was by Shawna. Frequently, for the truth to come into the heart and dwell there, several weeks of study and contemplation are necessary. If we expect quality learning to occur, time must be given to allow the truth of God's Word to penetrate. It is only as learners come to understand that Scripture is for them that they begin to see and sense their personal responsibility for obedience.

Allowing time in the class session for questions between the teacher and child gives a signal that believers don't have to swallow the whole of Scripture without chewing on it piece by piece. Children need to interact with their peers about substantive issues, and the classroom is an ideal place for this to occur. For some reason, many teachers believe that learning takes place only in a classroom where silence reigns, and they spend valuable time trying to maintain quiet classes. I believe, however, that classes with a low level of noise are probably more conducive to learning. Very little learning is likely to take place when the teacher is the only one talking.

Kohlberg, whose study in moral development has influenced the educational scene for decades, reminds teachers that interaction is a necessity among children. In order to move successfully through the stages of moral development, children need to discuss life dilemmas they encounter with someone who is at a higher stage. If our desire is for them to think and behave with greater moral intent, then opportunities must be provided for interaction in the classroom. Perhaps volunteer teachers are fearful they will lose control of the class if they allow children to interact, but that is a risk that must be taken if our classrooms are to be conducive to interaction and learning. Children need to experiment with their ideas in a safe environment before they try them out on people outside the confines of the classroom. That's what Shawna was doing in the conversation with her teacher. She was questioning her understanding of what was required in being a "good Samaritan" and then determining a course of action by seeking the affirmation of the adult in the class.

Sometimes questioning is a skill that teachers need to develop to reinforce the learning that has taken place. In a seminar, I observed a master teacher at work with a small group of children. I was sure she had taken Questioning 101 in college! She asked a few factual questions but primarily she asked affective questions like, "How do you think Moses felt when he stretched the rod out over the Red Sea and it parted?" Some questions she asked the children caused them to reflect on the events of the story and put themselves in the place of the primary characters. "What would you do if you found an injured dog at the side of the road?" By asking nonfactual questions and listening to the children's responses, a teacher helps children verbalize their thoughts, which is helpful for both teacher and student. One question may lead to another, which can clarify a learner's thinking and stimulate learning in the class as a whole.

Reinforcement of learning may also occur through other activities, such as having a child summarize the story for the day. In her workshops, Madeline Hunter uses an effective reinforcer by asking the learner, "What is the most important thing you have learned today?" The responses to that question are as varied as the learners in the group, and their answers are always interesting for the teacher to contemplate.

Educational Foundation for Practical Application

In the appropriating phase of the learning process, the internalization of learning is accomplished. Quality communication between teachers and learners enhances this phase. In communication theory, we learn a helpful equation: perception + thinking = communication.[4] Perception is frequently unconscious and occurs through the senses: seeing, hearing, touching, smelling, and tasting. "We use these representations to make meaning of the real world in a process called thinking."[5]

There are three primary representational systems: visual (sight), auditory (sound), and kinesthetic (touch). We do not function in only one system because much depends on the context and situation around us. Children who perceive sights, sounds, and smells around them store these memories in their minds in pictures. We call them visual learners. They prefer pictures and written words to other forms of instruction and rely heavily upon these modes to gain information.[6]

When I was a little girl, my grandmother desperately wanted me to learn to crochet. Together we sat on the swing with crochet needle and thread in hand. Grandma would show me how to hold the thread and what to do with the needle, but for some reason, I could not master the art. (At eight years of age, lack of intrinsic motivation might also have contributed to that inability to learn!)

Some time later after my grandmother was no longer living, I decided I wanted to learn to crochet. I went to the craft store and bought an instruction booklet that contained visual instructions and diagrams for the process. Wonder of wonders, this time I was able to read the words and perform the various motions required for each stitch.

Visual learners need to personally read Scripture to internalize the information adequately. They need to read the instructions for activities on a task card or from the curriculum piece. This helps them to absorb the detail of what is to be accomplished.

Auditory learners prefer sounds to pictures. They are capable of hearing instructions and of doing the activities. It is not nearly as important for them to personally read Scripture as it is for visual learners. They merely have to hear the words and to take in the message.

Kinesthetic learners are more aware of tactile sensations than they are of either pictures or sounds. They depend upon their feelings to help them in the learning process. They must "be in touch with" the activity and need to "do something" with whatever is being learned.[7]

> What does all this have to do with effective learning? Teachers need to be aware that these representational systems are operating in their classroom and need to be accommodated if learning is to be efficient and comfortable for the various learners. The teacher needs to provide instruction, activities, and reinforcement that will match each child's primary representational system. If communication is the goal of our teaching, we need to match the way we do things in the classroom with the way children perceive.

A speaker once compared the task of communicating in representational systems to the attempt to telephone a friend whose number you did not know. You can continually dial a series of seven numbers and ultimately you will reach the person, because there is a limited number of combinations that can be used. But if you know the person's phone number, you can dial it easily and connect yourself with the friend. An instant connection is what is sought in asking teachers to communicate with learners in their primary representational system. Tapping into the learner's system increases the effectiveness of the communication.

Another influence on the appropriating phase of the learning process is brain modality. "The human brain is the most highly organized and complex structure in the known universe."[8] The structure of the brain cortex is bilaterally symmetrical.

> Each cortical hemisphere is composed of four major regions or lobes. These are named frontal, parietal, temporal, and occipital lobes. While it is clear that these lobes do not act as independent functional units, (most higher level functions are known to be distributed across more than one region of the cortex), it is still the case that many human attributes and functions appear to be strongly associated with a single lobe.

> The frontal lobes appear to be associated with initiative, anticipation, caution, and the general regulation and planning of action; the temporal lobes with the integration of perceptual information, especially speech and vision; the parietal lobes with symbolic processes (reading, writing, arithmetic), spatial perception, and motor control; and the occipital lobes with vision, the dominant sense in humans and other primates.[9]

Given that these are the functions of the brain, how does brain modality affect learning? Research findings on right and left brain functions have been released in the last two decades. They are simultaneously exciting, fascinating, and controversial. But then so initially were Piaget and his studies. Christian educators need to be cognizant of this research and of its potential impact on learning and instruction. They need to be prepared to incorporate these concepts into their teaching methodologies.

Brain modality has been commonly referred to as "right brain," "left brain," and "whole brain," and they function in very different mental areas.

> In most people the left side of the brain deals with logic, language, reasoning, number, linearity, and analysis etc., the so called "academic" activities. While the left side of the brain is engaged in these activities, the right side is in the "alpha wave" or resting stage. The right side of the brain deals with rhythm, music, images and imagination, colour, parallel processing, daydreaming, face recognition, and pattern or map recognition.[10]

Our two brains are linked by the corpus callosum, which is a concentration of nerve fibers. It is through this cluster of nerve fibers that the two hemispheres communicate.[11] Because of this link, we can operate as whole-brained individuals functioning to the peak of our human potential.

Each individual has a preference for a primary functioning brain hemisphere and needs to develop the other, although each is equally important in learning. With the left side associated with analytical thinking and the right side being intuitive and creative, learners need to experience activities that incorporate both hemispheres of the brain.

McCarthy has a wonderful summary of how these research findings relate to learning:

> The left and right hemispheres of the brain
> process information and
> experience differently.
>
> The left brain does verbal things.
> The left brain likes sequence.
> The left brain sees the trees.
> The left brain is structured.
> School is for the left brain.
> Schools do not teach to the right brain.
>
> The right does visual-spatial things.
> The right likes random patterns.
> The right sees the forest.
> The right is fluid and spontaneous.
>
> How fortunate for students who are left mode dominant.
> How sad for students who are right mode dominant.
>
> People who are left mode dominant have beautiful gifts.
> They are systematic,
> they solve problems by looking at the parts,
> they are sequential and are excellent planners,
> they are analytic.
>
> People who are right mode dominant have beautiful gifts.
> They see patterns,
> they solve problems by looking at the whole picture,
> they are random and arrive at accurate conclusions in the absence
>   of logical justification,
> they are intuitive.[12]

As Christian educators, we need to appreciate the whole of God's creation in our learners and teach in a wholistic approach that will accommodate children who prefer one hemisphere to the other. Again, McCarthy summarizes how teachers might accomplish this:

> We need to lecture and interact,
> to show them how and to let them try it,
> to have them memorize and learn to question the experts,

to give answers and ask better questions,
to train their minds and value responses from their hearts,
to solve problems and to find problems,
to train the intellect and the imagination,
to hold on to our best traditional techniques and to add new ones,
to teach them the best that civilization offers,
and give them the courage and confidence to adapt and grow.[13]

Christian educators need to dispense with some traditional teaching methods if we expect learners to become adept in appropriating through the learning process.

Like Paul to the church at Colossae, we need to help our children discover and appropriate the truth that they are the riches of the kingdom, "which is Christ in you, the hope of glory." Then our teaching goals can become "teaching everyone with all wisdom, so that we may present everyone perfect in Christ" (Col. 1:27–28).

ENDNOTES

[1]John W. Gardner, *Self-Renewal: The Individual and the Innovative Society* (New York: Harper & Row, 1963), 21–22.

[2]Adapted from International Center for Learning. Ventura, Calif.: Gospel Light Publications. Used by permission of the publisher.

[3]Iris Cully, *Christian Child Development* (San Francisco: Harper & Row, 1979).

[4]Genie Z. Laborde, *Influencing with Integrity: Management Skills for Communication and Negotiation* (Palo Alto, Calif.: Syntony, 1983).

[5]Laborde, *Influencing with Integrity*, 68.

[6]Ibid.

[7]Ibid.

[8]Martin A. Fischler and Oscar Firschein, *Intelligence: The Eye, The Brain, and the Computer* (Reading, Mass.: Addison-Wesley, 1987), 23.

[9]Ibid., 30.

[10]Tony Buzan, *Use Both Sides of Your Brain* (New York: E. P. Dutton, 1983), 14.

[11]Jacquelyn Wonder and Priscilla Donovan, *Whole-Brained Thinking: Working From Both Sides of the Brain to Achieve Peak Job Performance* (New York: Ballantine, 1984).

[12]Bernice McCarthy, *The 4MAT System: Teaching to Learning Styles with Right/Left Mode Techniques* (Barrington, Ill.: EXCEL, 1980), 75. Used by permisssion of the author.

[13]Ibid., 77.

ADDITIONAL RESOURCES

Anderson, John R., ed. *Cognitive Skills and Their Acquisition*. Hillsdale, N.J.: Lawrence Erlbaum Associates, 1981.

Bandura, Albert, and Robert Jerry. "Role of Symbolic Coding and Rehearsal Processes in Observational Learning" *Journal of Personality and Social Psychology*, 26, no. 1 (1973): 273–84.

Blakeslee, Thomas R. *The Right Brain*. Garden City, N.Y.: Doubleday, 1980.

Bogen, Joseph E. "Some Educational Aspects of Hemispheric Specialization." *UCLA Educator*, 17 (1975): 24–32.

Brown, George I. *Human Teaching for Human Learning: An Introduction to Confluent Education*. New York: Viking, 1971.

Buzan, Tony. *Make the Most of Your Mind*. New York: Linden Press/Simon & Schuster, 1984.

Edwards, Betty. *Drawing on the Right Side of the Brain*. Los Angeles: J. P. Tarcher, 1979.

Flavell, John H. *Cognitive Development*, 2d ed. Englewood Cliffs, N.J.: Prentice-Hall, 1985.

————. *The Developmental Psychology of Jean Piaget*. New York: D. Van Nostrand, 1963.

Gardner, Howard. *The Mind's New Science: A History of Cognitive Revolution*. New York: Basic, 1985.

Gattegno, Caleb. *What We Owe Children: Subordination of Teaching to Learning*. New York: Outerbridge, 1970.

Goleman, Daniel. "People Who Read People." *Psychology Today* (July 1979).

Von Oech, Roger. *A Whack on the Side of the Head*. New York: Warner, 1983.

Ostrander, Sheila and Lynn Schroeder. *Super-Learning*. New York: Dell, 1979.

Sperry, Roger W. "Lateral Specialization of Cerebral Function in the Surgically Separated Hemispheres." *The Neurosciences Third Study Program*, eds. F. O. Schymitt and R. G. Worden, Cambridge, Mass.: Massachusetts Institute of Technology Press, 1974: 5–9.

Springer, Sally P., and Georg Deutsch. *Left Brain, Right Brain*. San Francisco: W. H. Freeman, 1985.

Chapter 5

Life-Changing Behavior

The spiritual goal of the learning process is to have children adopt patterns of behaviors that are Christlike. If teachers do not expect and pray for their learners to change, then why teach? "The spiritual person and the spiritual community are both agents of formation, but they accomplish this formation most completely when there is a conscious effort to assist individuals in the development of the spiritual life."[1]

Spiritual formation is a primary teaching goal. Christian educators want children to come to know Jesus Christ as Savior, but that is only the beginning of the Christian walk. The Sunday school class and other programs in the church can help the child understand Christian community, but each child must also begin to take personal responsibility for responses, actions, and behavior. The learner controls the spiritual formation that occurs, although teachers, parents, peers, church leaders, children's programs, and, supremely, the Holy Spirit have an impact on the process. "As teachers, we prepare, pray, and teach, but God is the only One who can effect life change."[2]

ASSUMING RESPONSIBILITY

There is a saying, "God has only children and no grandchildren." That is to remind us that the Christian life is one of *personal* pursuit, response, and responsibility, and that as individuals we receive our heavenly reward. No one else can do it for us.

In Figure 11 below, the progression of the learning process can be observed.

Figure 11
The Learning Process[3]
(Assuming Responsibility)

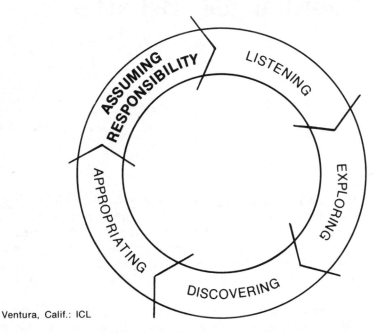

Ventura, Calif.: ICL

Having arrived at the final phase, we begin to see how the whole cycle works. Children *listen* to teachers of God's Word, then *explore* the concepts firsthand in Scripture. With the exploration comes the joy of making personal *discoveries* related to the material. At this juncture, the learner makes a conscious or unconscious decision that, "Yes, this was written for me" and then *appropriates* or internalizes the message. The final phase of **assuming responsibility** for that which is learned is the ultimate goal of the learning process.

Traditional classroom teachers in the church often believe that learners listen to what is being said and automatically assume responsibility for the desired, changed behavior. This is possible, but when it occurs as a result of this type of teaching, it is likely to be only short-term learning.

Recall the example given in Chapter 1 about the church that was pursuing substantial increases in its missionary funding. The first year in their mission conference, the speaker's message evoked a positive financial response that lasted about three months. This is an example of short-term learning. But when the church leaders respected the individuals' learning processes and scheduled opportunities for questions and interaction after the speaker's presentation, learners explored, discovered, and appropriated the message. This resulted in their assuming long-term responsibility for changed behavior in their giving patterns.

Biblical Principles

Children need to learn that God loves them above all things in creation. They were loved so much that Jesus Christ died on the cross for their sins. When children are convinced that this is true, they will ultimately confess love, faith, and trust in him. But belief in Christ also elicits a response of obedience to him and his Word. This obedience is seen in a desire to walk in a manner worthy of the calling, to be one of Christ's disciples and servants.

These are abstract concepts that represent the direction of the spiritual walk. But a child's ability to grasp them will depend on her or his age and developmental maturity. This is the reason churches need Christian teachers who can become models, spiritual directors, and instruments of the Holy Spirit to facilitate the spiritual growth of the child.

Children who have become believers in Christ as Savior need to realize that they are no longer individuals pursuing their own goals. Now they are "adopted sons and daughters" of his with new allegiances and responsibilities for service.

> For Christ's love compels us, because we are convinced that one died for all, and therefore all died. And he died for all, that those who live *should no longer live for themselves,* but for him who died for them and was raised again. . . . We are therefore Christ's ambassadors, as though God were making his appeal through us . . . so that in him we might become the righteousness of God. (2 Cor. 5:14–15, 20–21, italics mine)

Believers become his ambassadors and representatives to all humanity. "To love in accordance with Christ's commandment, one must actually *overcome* basic human nature. For Christ's view of love involves believing, giving, and serving. By contrast, human nature's brand of love involves receiving and dominating."[4]

Becoming giving and serving disciples of Christ requires that the child assume responsibility for changing behaviors in accordance with God's Word. "Whatever happens, conduct yourselves in a manner worthy of the gospel of Christ . . ." (Phil. 1:27). The desire of Christian educators is that their learners choose to become believers in God's redemption, receive the gift of salvation, and serve him forever. "Whatever you do, work at it with all your heart, as working for the Lord, not for men, since you know that you will receive an inheritance from the Lord as a reward. It is the Lord Christ you are serving" (Col. 3:23–24).

It is the Lord Christ whom we serve, and he desires and deserves the very best we can produce.

Practical Application

The end product of the fifth and final phase in the learning process is that children assume responsibility for their actions as a response to Scripture. Let's refer to Shawna's experience, outlined in Chapter 4.

When a child realizes in studying the story of the good Samaritan that there are personal applications for those ideas, this shows the child's ability to identify with another (or social perspective-taking). This means that he or she can incorporate some changes in behavior toward others. In this case, Shawna appropriated the biblical lesson into her life. She had learned that the lesson was for her and that there were some things she needed to do to apply it to her personal life.

The next step in the process for Shawna is to begin searching for ways to act on her learning. She must do more than talk to her teacher about her discovery. She needs to begin to assume responsibility for her learning by living it out on the playground, in the school classroom, and in the neighborhood. There are several ways that Shawna can become a good Samaritan to Judy. She could give her some of her clothes, she could talk to her about brushing her hair and washing her face before school, she could tutor her in math, she could defend Judy when other children talk about her, and she could work at becoming a friend to Judy.

Assuming responsibility in the learning process means that the learner will do something overt that manifests the inner change. Thinking and behavior will likely change if learning has taken place.

Another goal Christian educators might have for their learners is that they become self-disciplined in life. Jeremy, a fourth grader, was reading for his Sunday school class Matthew 22:33–40, the passage where the lawyer questioned Jesus about the greatest commandment. Actually, in this passage Jesus gave two commandments: the first being to love the Lord with all your heart, soul, and mind, and the second being to love your neighbor as yourself.

Jeremy, a recipient of God's grace in redemption, had listened to what the teacher was saying about love being important in all of life. The curriculum had incorporated several contemporary stories about people loving one another, and as he explored these with his classmates, he began to discover (with the help of the teacher's questioning) the common thread of love as the motivator for doing things for others. When he began to appropriate and internalize this truth, he made a list of things he could do at home and school that would illustrate his obedience to the two greatest commandments Jesus gave. But not until he began to practice the items on the list could we feel that he had learned what it means to love others as himself.

No one can force or coerce a child into assuming responsibility for applying these commandments to life. Adult pressure may force a superficial obedience, but a child must be intrinsically motivated to do it or not to do it. Self-discipline, through the power of the Holy Spirit, is the attribute that actually brings about the life-change in behavior. In James 1:22–27, we are reminded that just hearing the Word and planning to do something about it is not sufficient. We are to be doers of the Word, assuming responsibility for the actions Scripture convinces us to incorporate into our daily living.

Educational Foundation for Practical Application

Educators have known for decades that parents are the most significant and influential teachers of children. By the age of six, children have formed many of the concepts that will be with them throughout their adult lives. The early childhood years are vital contributors to the development of adult attitudes and perspectives.[5]

An interesting phenomena observed about recent Christian literature is that it ignores or only acknowledges in passing the contributions of major theorists and researchers who have studied the psychosexual and/or psychosocial development that influence adult attitudes. One can only speculate why there is such a void in this area. Perhaps it is due to the evangelical world's disdain for any writing that alludes to evolutionary or humanistic thought.

Certainly Christian educators need to be cautious about what they accept as truth. However, they shouldn't "throw the baby out with the bath water." They need to be aware of what secular research has given us—a whole range of different ways that children grow and develop. This is essential if the child is to be educated wholistically.

One example is Erik Erikson's work. Erikson is a humanistic psychologist who developed a theory of psychosocial developmental tasks that take a lifetime to accomplish. This theory needs to be studied because there appears to be a correlation between the development of psychosocial relationships and the child's ability, desire, and capacity for assuming responsibility in personal application of biblical truth. Erikson reminds us that all humans have at least one thing in common: we all started life as babies.[6] He describes his work as a "conceptual itinerary," giving shape to the journey we all make. His work emerged from a comprehensive knowledge of Sigmund and Anna Freud's research in psychoanalysis. The Freuds' studies of adults helped them develop a new way of looking at childhood. "We have a name for the pressure of excessive wishes (the 'id') and for the oppressive force of conscience (the 'superego') . . . if we try to define the state of relative equilibrium between the well-known extremes . . . the ego dwells."[7] The ego, for Erikson, provided that "order within individuals on which all outer order depends."[8]

Robert Coles succinctly summarizes the research of Freud and Erikson.

> Freud once and for all proved the adult is still in many respects a child. Erikson said yes, that is true, and so true that it also works the other way: children have within them forecasts and forebodings of the future. They have "libido" and strong (possessive or angry) feelings toward their parents; but they also have what grown-up people have—an ear for what the neighbors believe or oppose, an eye for how one ought to dress, a sense of what should be done with the hours of the day, a feeling for people and places.[9]

While the Freuds studied adult, childless, female subjects, Erikson, through observational research methods, studied children at play. Erikson believed that play is to childhood what work is to the adult. Children invest their entire "energies, enthusiasms and disappointments" in play.[10] Through these observational research methods, Erikson developed a model he called the "epigenetic diagram."

> "Epi" means "upon"; and "genesis" "emergence." So epigenesis means that one time develops on top of another in space and time, and this seemed to me a simple enough configuration to be adopted for our purposes. But, of course, I extended it to include a hierarchy of stages, not just a sequence.[11]

This model later became known as the eight stages of man. A diagram of the model is reproduced in Figure 12.

In this diagram the sequence of stages and their hierarchical relationship are visible. It is interesting to note that in Erikson's own writing about the stages, the discussion begins with the top line of the chart on integrity vs. despair, disgust. Logically, this should signal to the reader that achieving the virtue of wisdom in old age depends heavily upon the successful integration of all the previous stages, beginning in infancy with trust vs. mistrust.[12]

Erikson believes that a possible fixation between any of these stages can contribute to developmental arrest at some point in time.[13]

Figure 12
Erikson's Eight States of Man

Psychosocial Crises

	1	2	3	4	5	6	7	8
Old Age VIII								Integrity vs. Despair, Disgust. WISDOM
Adulthood VII							Generativity vs. Stagnation. CARE	
Young Adulthood VI						Intimacy vs. Isolation. LOVE		
Adolescence V					Identity vs. Identity Confusion. FIDELITY			
School Age IV				Industry vs. Inferiority. COMPETENCE				
Play Age III			Initiative vs. Guilt. PURPOSE					
Early Childhood II		Autonomy vs. Shame, Doubt. WILL						
Infancy I	Basic Trust vs. Mistrust. HOPE							

Figure 12. Reproduced from *The Life Cycle Completed: A Review* by Erik H. Erikson, by permission of W. W. Norton & Company, Inc. Copyright © 1982 by Rikan Enterprises Ltd.

These disruptions in the normal flow of development can become serious enough to require counseling and perhaps, ultimately, psychoanalysis.

In Figure 12, note the contrasting terms used to define the actions of each stage and the end product or virtue (as Erikson calls it) derived from successful integration: trust vs. mistrust, resulting in HOPE; autonomy vs. shame, doubt, resulting in WILL; initiative vs. guilt, resulting in PURPOSE, etc. For the Christian educator to fully comprehend the intricacies of these ideas and to appreciate their impact upon child development and Christian education, Erikson's books and articles must be read. His emphasis on the link between cognitive, psychosocial, psychosexual and moral development are thought-provoking for the Christian educator.

The rationale for incorporating, highlighting, and exploring all of the educational, psychological, and learning theories in this volume is to underscore the point that assuming responsibility for changed behavior completes the learning process, yet is heavily dependent upon the child's ability to integrate all of life's relationships and experiences into a coherent whole. This is no small accomplishment for the child. The Christian educator needs to keep these theories in view when planning and designing programs for children.

The goal of Part I of this text is to whet the reader's appetite with just enough information to entice the adult learner into pursuing these subjects further. Perhaps something has been included with which you disagree. Great! Get into the literature and search for your answers firsthand.

The list of additional resources at the end of each chapter suggests where to begin the search for more information. The learning process as described in this text applies to adult learners as well as to children. The concept in Scripture of the priesthood of believers applies to educational knowledge just as it does to biblical information. Each believer who has the desire to know more and has the motivation to pursue it can become competent and responsible for the pursuit of knowledge.

As Paul prayed for the Ephesians, I also pray for readers:

> I pray also that the eyes of your heart may be enlightened in order that you may know the hope to which he has called you, the riches of his glorious inheritance in the saints, and his incomparably great power for us who believe. . . . For we are God's workmanship, created in Christ Jesus to do good works, which God prepared in advance for us to do. (Eph. 1:18–19; 2:10)

As teachers desiring to develop Christlike children, let us set about our task with as much biblical and educational knowledge as can be gained.

ENDNOTES

[1]Iris V. Cully, *Education for Spiritual Growth* (San Francisco: Harper & Row, 1984), 31.

[2]Terry Hall, *How to Be the Best Sunday School Teacher You Can Be* (Chicago: Moody Press, 1986), 118.

[3]Adapted from International Center for Learning (Ventura, Calif.: Gospel Light). Used by permission of the publisher.

[4]Gail and Gordon MacDonald, *If Those Who Reach Could Touch* (Old Tappan, N.J.: Revell, 1984), 20.

[5]David Elkind, *The Child and Society: Essays in Applied Child Development* (New York: Oxford University Press, 1979).

[6]Erik H. Erikson, *Childhood and Society,* 2d ed. (New York: W. W. Norton, 1963).

[7]Ibid., 192–93.

[8]Ibid., 194.

[9]Robert Coles, *Erik H. Erikson: The Growth of His Work* (Boston: Little, Brown and Co., 1970), 79.

[10]Ibid., 132.

[11]Richard I. Evans, *Dialogue with Erik Erikson* (New York: Harper & Row, 1967), 21–22.

[12]Erik H. Erikson, *The Life Cycle Completed: A Review* (New York: W. W. Norton, 1982), 56–57. Reproduced by permission of W. W. Norton & Company, Inc. Copyright © 1982 by Rikan Enterprises Ltd.

[13]Evans, *Dialogue with Erik Erikson.*

ADDITIONAL RESOURCES

Beadle, Muriel. *A Child's Mind: How Children Learn During The Critical Years From Birth to Age Five.* Garden City, N.J.: Doubleday, 1970.

Bloom, Benjamin, ed. *Taxonomy of Educational Objectives, Handbook I: Cognitive Domain.* New York: McKay, 1956.

Bolton, Barbara. *Creative Bible Learning: For Children Grades One to Six.* Ventura, Calif.: Regal, 1977.

————. *How to Do Bible Learning Activities: Grades 1–6.* Ventura, Calif.: International Center for Learning, 1982.

Bolton, Barbara, Charles T. Smith, and Wes Haystead. *Everything You Want to Know About Teaching Children (Grades 1–6).* Ventura, Calif.: Gospel Light, 1987.

Damon, William. *The Social World of the Child.* San Francisco: Jossey-Bass, 1977.

Duska, Ronald, and Mariellen Whelan. *Moral Development: A Guide to Piaget and Kohlberg.* New York: Paulist, 1975.

Elkind, David. *Children and Adolescents.* New York: Oxford, 1970.

Fraiberg, Selma. *The Magic Years.* New York: Scribner, 1959.

Freud, Sigmund. *A General Introduction to Psychoanalysis.* New York: Washington Square, 1960.

Harrell, Donna, and Wesley Haystead. *Creative Bible Learning: For Young Children Birth–5 Years.* Ventura, Calif.: Regal, 1977.

Hartshorne, H., and M. May. *Studies in the Nature of Character, vols. 1, 2, 3.* New York: Macmillan, 1928–30.

Hoffman, Martin L. "Development of Moral Thought, Feeling, and Behavior." *American Psychologist* 34, no. 10 (1979): 956–65.

Klein, Karen. *How to Do Bible Learning Activities: Ages 2–5.* Ventura, Calif.: International Center for Learning, 1982.

Kuhmerker, Lisa, Marcia Mentoknowski, and V. Lois Erickson. *Evaluating Moral Development and Evaluating Education Programs That Have a Value Dimension.* Schenectady, N.Y.: Character Research, 1980.

Loevinger, Jane. "Ego Maturity and Human Development." *Developmental Theory and Its Application in Guidance Programs: Systematic Efforts to Promote Personal Growth.* Ed. G. Dean Miller, St. Paul, Minn.: Minnesota Department of Education, 1977.

Mussen, Paul, and Nancy Eisenberg-Berg. *Roots of Caring, Sharing, and Helping: The Development of Prosocial Behavior in Children.* San Francisco: W. H. Freeman, 1977.

Peddiwell, J. A. *The Saber-Tooth Curriculum.* New York: McGraw-Hill, 1939.

PART II
Teaching Effectively in the Classroom

... Good teaching is impossible, but *some* teachers teach well; but these teachers do it in completely different ways, and yet there must be some stateable principles we can find.[1]

Defining what constitutes good teaching is a difficult task. Agreeing with others on the goals of Christian education and instruction would be equally difficult; however, throughout Part I a list of "wants" for children was mentioned. The following areas of growth, not listed in any hierarchical or sequential order, are thought by many to influence an adult's life-long walk with Christ. Christian educators, therefore, want children to:

- grow into Christlikeness
- imitate Christ's love
- increase in wisdom
- increase in physical and moral attainment
- be acceptable to peers and other adults
- receive the gift of salvation and be nurtured and discipled in the faith
- develop critical thinking skills
- attain confidence in problem-solving
- become competent and capable
- be productive and contributing members of society
- become familiar with the Bible and its contents
- know God, to pursue an intimate relationship with him and to serve him forever
- come to know Jesus as Savior and Lord
- become self-disciplined in their approach to life.

By keeping these "wants" for children in the forefront of our planning and by learning how to teach effectively, teachers can help the children learn. Approaches to teaching are as numerous as teachers in the classroom. There is no *one* way to teach effectively.

Studies have examined the personality traits of teachers, the relationship between students and teachers, the classroom environment and climate, and countless other contributors to the teaching/learning process. But no single component can be conclusively determined to guarantee effective teaching.

Nonetheless, in Part II we will explore several key factors in effective teaching, such as biblical self-image, characteristics of effective teachers, planning the teaching sessions, and preparing effective lessons. This will establish the basic "HOW" of teaching more effectively.

Chapter 6

Influences on Classroom Environment

Childhood is a most formative and critical period for the development of adult concepts. Teachers can have a positive impact on this developmental process by providing a learning climate that is conducive to positive exploration and experiences.

ACQUIRING A BIBLICAL SELF-IMAGE

Scene 1. Susan arrives at the door of her Sunday school classroom. As she hugs the doorsill on her way into the room, her teacher greets her, "Good morning Susan. How are you this morning?" That's a standard salutation, but Susan ignores the question and hurries to the table activities. Her eyes are fixed on the floor from the minute she enters the room. Seldom does she even look at another person (child or adult) eye-to-eye.

Scene 2. When Matt's folks drop him off at Sunday school, he slams the car door and hustles himself into the church building. He literally bounds into the room, much like Superman, ready for the action of the day. As he seats himself at the table, he listens intently to a conversation in progress and then interrupts with, "Are you kidding? I could beat that guy easy. If he can score once, I can do it six times—blindfolded!"

Scene 3. The speaker at an adult luncheon begins his address by stating, "You are created in God's image. How can you, therefore, view yourself as inadequate, less than desirable, or an inferior, worthless product? But that's precisely how many people view themselves . . . inadequate, inferior, and worthless."

Each of these vignettes forces us to recall individuals from our past and our present. Low self-image is an epidemic of staggering proportions at all age levels of our society. In the opening chapter of James Dobson's book *Hide or Seek*, the life of one person with a low self-image—Lee Harvey Oswald—is recounted. It is a sad and sordid tale with an almost predictable outcome of anti-social behavior. But who would have guessed that such a man could alter the course of modern history with one bullet placed into the heart of a nation?

Did low self-image cause this unbelievable event? No one can say with certainty. But at least it contributed to an event that left a country of people stunned, fearful, and ultimately angry. How could this happen in 1963 in the United States of America—a country impervious to attack from without but exploited from within by a citizen with a low view of himself?

Self-esteem is defined by Stanley Coopersmith as:

> the evaluation which the individual makes and customarily maintains with regard to himself [herself]. It expresses an attitude of approval, and indicates the extent to which the individual believes himself [herself] to be capable, significant, successful, and worthy.[2]

Research literature uses a variety of labels almost interchangeably to express one's view of self: self-perception, self-worth, self-awareness, self-respect, self-love, self-esteem, and self-image. I have selected the term self-image to use throughout this section as I believe it is the most biblical of the available choices.

Is low self-image a virus being communicated to our children? Yes—it infects so quietly and so quickly that it is scarcely noticed. Even in an all-American sport like baseball, incidents that strike blows at the heart of self-image occur. When our son began to play Little League baseball, the fans who attended the games were primarily parents and grandparents. What harm would they do their own children? The answer is embedded in this poem given to new Little League parents and written by an unknown author:

> He stands at the plate with his heart pounding fast.
> The bases are loaded. The die has been cast.
> Mom and Dad cannot help him; he stands all alone.
> A hit at this moment would send his team home.
> The ball nears the plate. He swings and misses.
> There's a groan from the crowd—some boos and hisses.
> A thoughtless voice cries, "Strike out the bum!"
> Tears fill his eyes; the game's no longer fun.
> Remember, he's just a little boy who stands all alone

Trying his best for "the folks back home."
So open your heart and give him a break;
For it's moments like this a man you can make.
And keep this in mind when you hear someone forget—
He's just a little boy and not a man yet.

Can you sense the hurt and panic in this batter's heart when the pitcher's Dad (most likely) yells, "Strike out the bum!"? The pitcher's parents only want to support their child's effort, unfortunately at the expense of another child. How can this young batter already be a "bum"? What a price to pay for three successful pitches!

Society measures our worth and value by the grades we get, our athletic prowess, our musical expertise. Our identity is erroneously based on what we do. The pursuit of excellence has become a battle cry in this technological-informational age. But the pursuit of excellence in the secular classroom without a firm understanding of whose we are and why we are created will surely give rise to a generation of overachieving and emotionally empty adults.

Christians hold the antidote for the societal ill of low self-image. Proper biblical self-image is not achieved through praise, recognition, encouragement, or hourly warm-fuzzies. Rather, it is acquired through knowing that God created us in his image and for his purpose. Self-image, like salvation, is a gift from God. This has been true since creation. Scripture simply but profoundly states in Genesis 1:26–27 that the combined personality of the Trinity said, "Let us make man in our image, in our likeness. . . . So God created man in his own image, in the image of God he created him; male and female he created them."

ACCEPTING A BIBLICAL SELF-IMAGE

When one goes to the library to look up references on self-image, there are scores of books and journal articles available. Some titles concentrate on exterior reinforcers. These are the "building," "developing," or "positive-thinking" titles that underscore the behavioristic approaches to self-image. Behaviorists point to extrinsic sources for the motivation to achieve self-image because competence is one dimension of self-image.[3]

Self-image is affected by outside influences, but the personal view or internal perspective of self is the deeper and more penetrating way a biblical self-image is developed. Acceptance does not come from outside a person; rather, it is a personal, intrinsic choice to receive the gift of self-image given by God to each of us. "Christianity proclaims that the real basis of one's worth lies beyond one's accomplishments, even beyond good works. Ultimately it is God's love that grounds human dignity and the mature sense of self worth."[4] For the Christian child or adult, there should not have to be a discussion of high or low self-image. These are concepts thrust upon us by a narcissistic society that would have us dwell on external influences.

For the Christian, however, we must understand what it means to be created in God's image, beginning with the knowledge and acceptance of God's love and the value he places on us. The human race was not created by accident. It was a purposeful act of God. He looked around and viewed his creation and said, "It is very good" (Gen. 1:31). Surely he did not create us without proper self-image— the essential element in the establishment of all healthy relationships.[5] We did nothing to earn or lose self-image. It is God who creates us (in his image) and who molds and makes us the way we are. We should not question his divine intent. "The Christian self-image is ultimately based, not on our own achievements, but on God's gracious acceptance of us in Christ. . . . Our positive self-image, therefore, is not rooted in human merit but in divine grace."[6]

"But who are you, O man, to talk back to God? Shall what is formed say to him who formed it, 'Why did you make me like this?' Does not the potter have the right to make out of the same lump of clay some pottery for noble purposes and some for common use?" (Rom. 9:20–21). What arrogance is displayed when God's wisdom and purpose is questioned! I want to be taller . . . or more powerful . . . or influential . . . or _____ (you fill in a blank with your desire). God made us the way he intended. He committed no error in creation.

In my growing-up years I had one goal—to play basketball for the Hoosier Redheads, a woman's professional basketball team. As a guard, I practiced twenty-foot jump shots and foul shots, ad infinitum. At some point, however, it dawned on me that playing ball with that team was an unrealizable goal because I was 5'2" and had coal-black hair. The problem with the hair was not insurmountable, but the height I needed to play with the "big girls" was unobtainable. Surely God had made an error with me. Why would he have made me so short? He, obviously, had another plan for my life. It took me years to uncover that plan because I was so conscious of, and disgusted with, my height. That myopia hindered me from pursuing God's purpose for my life.

Just as God made no errors in creating us, neither did he make errors in the ordinal placement of children or in the specific household into which each child is born. Family members contribute significantly to the extrinsic view a child holds of him- or herself. Wayne Oates writes about families and their impact on a child's self-image:

You rather early found a part of your surroundings in life to be something you definitely did not like. You were repelled by it. You recoiled. You may have seen the treadmill way of life lived by your family of origin—your parents, brothers, sisters, uncles, aunts, and cousins. They took for granted the kind of work they were doing, the kind of values they cherished, the kind of hopes they were willing to settle for, and the way they used their minds and time. Not one of them ever considered, except in their dreams and imaginations, that there might be a different and even better way of life. They had no ambition to free themselves from the closed-in surroundings of the small town, the mill village, the mining community, the farm, the ghetto and living on welfare, etc. They felt themselves fated to be like this.

You loved them. You wanted them to have a better way of life. You wanted them to be ambitious like you were. You urged them to join you in your own ambitions for a good education, a larger world of interests, a freedom from slavery to an industrial or agricultural system that used people up in their bodily health and strength but provided no nurture for their mental and spiritual growth. Much to your surprise, they rejected you. They made fun of you and your ideas. They insisted on being "common folk," whereas you felt that they were more common than folk. So you became the odd ball. You launched out on your own without their blessing. You left them behind, feeling yourself a stranger to them. Thus, you could grow and survive even if they did not want to do so with you.[7]

Can you identify with children from homes like these?
Oates describes another kind of home and influence as follows:

You come from a background of great privilege, sophistication, and public trust. You have highly successful parents. Your brothers and sisters are high achievers in the worlds of the verbal, of status symbols, of ideas, of doing things in a proper and dignified manner. Very early you became uncomfortable with all this. You preferred to dress differently, to think differently, to use a very simple but blunt vocabulary. No college-professional route for your life! Rather, you chose to learn from direct experience. You were not a sit-at-home-and-talk kind. Abstractions were for persons who had little or no sense of life as it is really lived. You prefer to work with your hands. You do rather than say things.

Your parents used all their influence and money to "smooth the way" for you. You needed their help, yet you resented it. After a while—and it took you longer because you insisted on learning from direct experience rather than books, earning your way on personal merit rather than on diplomas, degrees, and certificates—your own native intelligence had its way. You became a self-made person after your own intuitive design. In fact, you probably did it the same way your father or mother did. You began to win in life. You were born, but not to lose. You were born to be you. Being you just took a little longer and was certainly an unpaved road to travel.[8]

These family descriptions represent only a couple of examples of how families influence children and their self-image. Families can have an impact on a child's view of self both positively and negatively. It is sometimes easier to blame others for a poor self-image but in order for growth to continue and as the child matures in development and spiritual faith, he or she must assume personal responsibility for self-image. Sometimes it is necessary as a first step to accepting oneself for an individual to forgive his or her parents for being fallible human beings.

Teachers also influence a child's view of self by what they choose to underscore in the classroom. What the teacher chooses to ignore or respond to in the classroom can either debilitate or support a child's view of self. The teacher's response sets the tone for how the peers will view the incident as well. When I was a first-grader, I accidentally knocked my crayons off my desk and they scattered all over the floor. The teacher reacted so violently to this that the whole class reminded me of my guilt for more than a week. I never forgot the lesson in "being perfect" that I received that day.

We can all dredge up events, situations, and relationships from our pasts that have been positive or negative influences on our self-image. The key here is to realize that in God alone, and through intrinsic acceptance of proper, biblical self-image, can the individual begin to comprehend who he or she is.

Children are created in God's image. It is only God who knows us deeply and as we really are. Though we are sinful people, it is incumbent upon us to see ourselves as God sees us—perfect and unblemished as a result of his plan of salvation granted through our Lord and Savior, Jesus Christ. We are children of the king—"adopted" sons and daughters—his redeemed creation (Eph. 1:5–12). God loved us so much before and after creation that he reconciled us to himself through the blood of his own Son (Col. 1:13–23).

It takes faith to believe that God exists, that Jesus Christ died for our sins, and that without this faith it is impossible to please him (Heb. 11:6). If we maintain a proper view of who God is (John 1:1–5) and his claim on our lives (John 1:12), how can we question our personal worth? We, adults and children, are his children—emotionally attached to God (Rom. 8:15), who will realize his plan through us. "The Lord will fulfill his purpose for me" (Ps. 138:8). "For the LORD of hosts has planned, and who can frustrate it?" (Isa. 14:27, NASB).

Plato's admonition to "know thyself" is, for the Christian, extremely good advice, because our self-image is based on our knowledge and acceptance of who we are as God's redeemed creation. Once we understand who we are and accept that God created us just the way we are, we must give him the glory (rather than the blame) for all that we are and all we accomplish through him.

Knowing who you are, whom you serve, and who gets the credit for what is done should liberate both the teacher and the learner to become more effective in their specific tasks of teaching and learning.

EFFECTIVE TEACHER CHARACTERISTICS

Educational research tells us that specific teacher traits of personality, motivation, education, and socio-economic levels contribute to effective teaching. However, there is *no one* trait or combination of traits that *guarantees* a teacher's success. Let's review a study that describes the kinds of things that effective teachers do in the classroom. This research was conducted in public schools, but application is easily made to the Christian education classroom.

Good, Grouws, and Ebmeia[9] were the researchers in this study. They observed six things that effective teachers do in the classroom:

1. *Effective teachers teach the class as a whole.* They do not single out a particular child and teach to that individual. Rather, through eye contact and a variety of questions, effective teachers help each child acquire a sense of belonging to the group. Often teachers are tempted to teach to the brightest child or the most disruptive child, but effective teachers teach the group and not a single individual.

This characteristic is consistent with Scripture—to be no respecter of persons, great or small. Surely it behooves the Christian educator to be accepting of all class members and treat them with equanimity.

2. *Effective teachers present information actively and clearly.* They involve learners early in the class period. These teachers are ready to begin class before the first learner arrives and they stress the objective of the lesson and the meaning of the material throughout the teaching session.

Jesus, the master teacher, was always ready, and he prepared the way for the disciples. When Jesus invited them to "Come, follow me," he immediately became the example for them. Scripture records that "Jesus went throughout Galilee, *teaching* in their synagogues, *preaching* the good news of the kingdom, and *healing* every disease and sickness among the people" (Matt. 4:23, emphasis mine). He was modeling his vision for ministry to his disciples.

3. *Effective teachers are task-focused.* They realize their teaching time is limited and consequently do not waste class time with nonessentials.

Christian educators have an extremely limited time in which to accomplish their goals. They must not waste it. Jesus also knew that his time on earth would be short; therefore, he taught his disciples with care, using concrete examples to cement their learning. Luke 5:5–11 contains the account of the men who fished all night but caught virtually nothing. When they obeyed his request to put their nets down in the deeper water, their nets were filled to the breaking point. The soon-to-be disciples learned that obedience precedes blessing, a lesson objective that Jesus underscored for them periodically.

4. *Effective teachers are basically nonevaluative and create a relaxed learning environment.* When children know that they belong to the group and that they are working cooperatively in the classroom, an environment that is conducive to quality learning exists. The teacher does not need to resort to praise or criticism but instead can become an encourager of every child's effort.

Jesus rebuked the disciples when they began to discuss which of them would be the greatest in the kingdom. He did not pat any of them on the back for what they had accomplished, but admonished them to be servants as he had been for them (Luke 22:24–27). Children need encouragement and models more than praise or criticism.

5. *Effective teachers express high achievement expectations.* Effective teachers desire and are able to secure a child's best effort by setting high standards of performance and by helping children confidently reach their potential. That is not to say that children are pressured to excel, but they are expected to do their very best in all areas.

In Luke 9:1–2, there is this account: "When Jesus had called the Twelve together, he gave them power and authority to drive out all demons and to cure diseases, and he sent them out to preach the kingdom of God and to heal the sick." Jesus had confidence in his band of learners, the disciples, and he had taught them well. They were expected to do as he had done. He modeled for them what to do and then he distributed the power and authority to accomplish the task. Should Christian educators do less?

6. *Effective teachers experience fewer discipline problems.* Classroom management in education is almost a discipline within the discipline. Much has been written about this topic because maintaining discipline in the classroom is critical to teaching and learning. Effective teachers who are able to accomplish all of the preceding

goals simply have fewer behavior challenges. Their learners feel a part of the class, they know they are all valued, that learning will take place, and that they are expected to do their best. In a classroom such as this, who would want to get into mischief or cause problems for other children?

PLANNING EFFECTIVE LESSONS

How can Christian educators plan the kind of lessons that will cause children to continue to grow and develop as the boy Jesus did (Luke 2:40)?

Madeline Hunter, an educator and researcher at UCLA, has given teachers some criteria to consider including in a lesson plan that should increase interest and effective learning.[10]

Anticipatory set. Effective teachers actively work at keeping a child involved in classroom activities. The purpose of the anticipatory set is to engage the thinking process and prepare the child for the content of the lesson. One method for doing this is to design a "hook" to get their minds thinking about the topic of the day. That "hook" can be in question format, with the teacher giving an example of a situation and then asking "Would that be fair?" Or the teacher might say, "Tell me about something unfair that happened to you this week," or ask "What does unfair mean?" The question would depend on the developmental level of the child. The "hook" can also be an activity such as drawing a picture of an unfair occurrence or writing a short story about the situation.

Purpose and objective. Knowing the purpose of the teaching unit and the objectives to be accomplished are central foci for effective teachers. As lessons are being planned, they keep these principles in the forefront of their preparation. Every activity, song, Scripture verse, or element of the teaching will reinforce the purpose and objective of the lesson.

Even to share the intent of the lesson with the learners is appropriate so that they know why the content is being studied. We should not teach lessons that have no ramifications for learning.

Instructional input. When teachers are using published curriculum, basic decisions have to be made regarding what part of the lesson to include. There is almost always more content included in the curriculum piece than can or should be included in one teaching session. The purpose of all this information is to allow the teacher to select those items of information appropriate for a particular group of children, considering their age level, needs, interests, and abilities.

In this portion of lesson planning, effective teachers have the opportunity and responsibility to include a variety of teaching styles, methodologies, and activities that together form the primary input for the session. Selecting a variety of instructional materials and teaching formats always keeps the learners anticipating what the teacher might do. Consider the following examples.

Think what excitement there would be in the class if Peter, dressed in his fisherman's attire, would come to the class and tell the Bible story. The Genesis Project has produced superb movies of portions of Scripture. Although expensive, the quality of dialogue in the language of the day and the scenery is unsurpassed. If your church has video equipment, rent an Ethel Barrett tape and let her keep your learners spellbound for twenty minutes!

The important thing is to make God's Word come alive for the class. There is no excuse for boring learners studying God's Word.

Modeling. Why should teachers expect their learners to be doing anything they are not also willing to do? Just as Jesus provided the example for his disciples, so do teachers need to live exemplary lives before their students. That is not to say that perfection is the goal, but teachers must be pursuing Christlikeness just as their learners are.

Jesus said and taught, "Can a blind man lead a blind man? Will they not both fall into a pit? A student is not above his teacher, but everyone who is fully trained will be like his teacher" (Luke 6:39–40). This is likely why in James 3:1 we are warned that not many should become teachers because they will incur a stricter judgment.

> Does that give you cause to consider who you are as Christ's ambassador in the classroom, in addition to what you teach and how you live?

Checking for understanding. Effective teachers want to know that their learners have understood the point and content of the lesson. The ability to ask good questions is developed as the teacher writes out some questions during the lesson planning stage. This preparation frequently helps to bring other questions to mind when the lesson is actually being taught.

As children respond to the questions, the teacher can listen for ideas they have gained that are not consistent with what is being taught. The opportunity to redirect a child's thinking while learning takes place is needed to assure that the child does not leave the room with misconceptions about the lesson.

Guided practice. The classroom is the place for a child to succeed or fail without suffering the consequences of ridicule and broken relationships that can result from failure in real life. To have opportunities to study and discuss biblical principles, and to consider and role-play how they apply to everyday life, gives the learner the chance to explore these issues in a safe climate.

Henrietta Mears, one of the founders of Gospel Light Publications, said, "The teacher hasn't taught until the learner has learned." If that is true, teachers need to take advantage of opportunities to guide children's thinking and practice and to encourage them always in Christlike behaviors and responses.

Independent practice. Effective teachers must develop confidence that what is being taught and how it is being done will ultimately produce learners who become like Christ. Learning without practicing what you know is like eating one potato chip—it can't be done!

In the classroom, the child may *listen* to the lesson, *explore* the Scripture provided, and even *discover* some hidden or obvious truth contained therein. But until the learner *appropriates* or internalizes the concept and then *assumes responsibility* for its implementation into real life situations, life-changing learning has not occurred. Children need to practice what they learn.

PREPARING EFFECTIVE LESSONS

Effective teachers need to consider when to incorporate all of the techniques listed previously when making their preparations for each class session. To prepare for teaching sessions properly and to avoid the rush of what is known as the "Saturday night scramble," teachers need to begin early in the week. The most important ingredient in lesson preparation is prayer. Pray to be used by God to meet the needs of those in your group, and then pray and expect changed lives as a result of what is being taught. We must always be aware that the Holy Spirit is the one causing the changes in children's lives that result from our teaching. "I [Paul] planted the seed, Apollos watered it, but God made it grow. So neither he who plants nor he who waters is anything, but only God, who makes things grow" (1 Cor. 3:6–7).

In your preparation, be aware of the purpose of the unit and the lesson aims and objectives as you begin to study. Read over these several times. Then study the scriptural basis for the lesson. Always read what God's Word has to say before you read what the editors have written. Sometimes God's Word stresses something the editor has omitted, and God's Word should be the textbook of the faith.

Once materials for other lesson activities are ready, your preparation is complete. It is now class time. **Never** take the curriculum piece into the room. Children, especially young ones, might believe that what you are teaching is coming from a storybook and is, therefore, fantasy rather than truth. They need to see you teach from and using the Bible and not the curriculum piece, as your teaching resource. That is not to say that pictures, or charts, or maps, or any other teaching aid should not be used; just center your teaching on God's Word. If you feel that you need more than your Bible, outline the lesson on a note card and tuck it into the Bible, but teach directly from God's Word.

Also, speak in a normal voice and communicate as one would with friends. Resist the temptation to "say it like the editor did" because editors write to be read and not recited, and they are not teaching your group of children. Additionally, very few curriculum writers can insert humor and occasionally a passage calls for some funny comments from the teacher.

To teach effectively, you need an anticipatory set or a "hook" to get the class's attention—some instructional input based on the teaching objectives, and an application to the students' lives to reinforce the learning. All this needs to happen in keeping with the learning process outlined in Part I.

Let's explore a sample fourth-grade-level lesson designed to involve learners throughout the session. The text for the lesson is Matthew 20:1-16. As the fourth-grade children arrive, they are asked to think about and either draw or write a response to the following questions: "What does 'unfair' mean?" or "What is the most unfair thing that happened to you this week?" or "How did you feel about the unfair event?" This questioning activity becomes the "hook" that captures their thoughts and in turn, directs their interest toward the concept for the session.

The content of the lesson could be initiated by a role-play. Have the learners mill around in the corner of the room and pretend they are in a marketplace. The teacher is the landowner and goes to the marketplace to hire laborers for the day. A price is negotiated with the first group and the landowner should flash a quarter (the denarius was worth about $.18) before them as a sign of their wages and then send them off to work.

Consistent with Scripture, go to the marketplace and select workers four more times during the day. On these trips don't negotiate the price; just tell them that you, the landowner, will pay them fairly for their labor. At the close of the day distribute the quarters to each worker, beginning with those who worked least. As the group who labored longest is paid a quarter and they watch and see that other groups receive the same, strange looks may begin to appear on their faces. Some may just shrug their shoulders, but others will be visibly shaken by what they consider to be an unfair wage, since they received the same as others who worked fewer hours. If the children are normal and honest, the "landowner" can expect from the first group of workers the same kind of grumbling that the Bible characters produced. They are thoroughly disgusted with this deal and you can tell it!

Now come back to the table and read the Bible story together so the children can see that this is a parable Jesus told to explain some things to them. Depending on the age of the child, this Bible story could focus on different issues. For young children (first and second grade), the fairness topic might be the focus for reinforcement. For middle children (third and fourth grade) the focus might be that this is what will happen to those who believe in Christ, regardless of when in their lives they come to that saving knowledge. They will all receive eternal life in heaven. For older children (fifth and sixth grades), the concept of God's grace toward each believer might be the focus.

Reinforcement and/or application activities should be a part of the lesson. An example of an application activity that would be appropriate for young children might be to explore a series of case studies describing dilemmas where fairness is at stake for them. For example, Tim has to do chores around the house—making his bed, feeding the dog, and taking out the trash. After his chores are done, his parents give him a weekly allowance. His friend Dan gets an allowance without having to do anything. Is this fair? Why or why not? Another example: Susan and Marie are caught by a grouchy neighbor riding their bikes through the yard. The neighbor calls Susan's mother to complain and request punishment, but does not call Marie's mother. Is that fair? Why or why not? Allowing them to discuss and react to the situations could be valuable as they begin verbalizing their views.

To reinforce the truth of eternal life to believers, the teacher might have children focus on people they love who are unbelievers. The teacher might explore with each individual child what he or she can do to retell this story to their friends and relatives.

Older children studying the grace of God might discuss receiving something they didn't deserve. Exploring ways they could serve others who hadn't earned the right to be served would be a valuable discussion, especially if concrete servant opportunities are outlined.

Throughout all the events and activities of this lesson, children need to have fellowship with one another. Sometimes we think that only adults need to have this, but time should be set aside so the children can get to know one another. If peer interaction is as important for moral development as Lawrence Kohlberg says, then time needs to be allotted for it to occur.

John R. W. Stott tells us that in preparing for anything there are four things we need to do: "fill full; think straight; pray hot; and let go!" This is fantastic advice for the Christian educator. Regardless of the age level to be taught, teachers should "fill full" on God's Word, "think straight" about what will be communicated and how it will be done in the session, "pray hot" to be available and used by the Holy Spirit, and "let go" with the prepared presentation, allowing yourself to be sensitive to the leading of the Holy Spirit as you move through the components of the teaching session.

ENDNOTES

[1]Peter Elbow, *Embracing Contraries: Explorations in Learning and Teaching* (New York: Oxford University Press, 1986), 141.

[2]Stanley Coopersmith, *The Antecedents of Self-Esteem* (San Francisco: W. H. Freeman, 1967), 4–5.

[3]S. Harter, "Competence as a Dimension of Self-Evaluation: Toward a Comprehensive Model of Self-Worth," in R. E. Leahy, ed., *The Development of the Self* (New York: Academic Press, 1985), 55–121.

[4]Evelyn Eaton Whitehead and James D. Whitehead, *Christian Life Patterns: The Psychological Challenges and Religious Invitations of Adult Life* (Garden City, N.Y.: Doubleday, 1979), 206.

[5]Keith Huttenlocker, *Becoming the Family of God: A Handbook for Developing Creative Relationships in the Church* (Grand Rapids: Zondervan, 1986).

[6]Anthony A. Hoekema, *Created in God's Image* (Grand Rapids: Eerdmans, 1986), 98.

[7]Wayne Oates, *Nurturing Silence in a Noisy Heart* (Garden City, N.Y.: Doubleday, 1979), 69. Used by permission of the author.

[8]Ibid., 70.

[9]Thomas L. Good, "Recent Classroom Research: Implications for Teacher Evaluation," *Essential Knowledge for Beginning Teachers,* David C. Smith, ed. (Washington, D.C.: American Association of Colleges for Teacher Education). As cited from Thomas L. Good, Douglas A. Grouws, and Howard Ebmeia, *Active Mathematics Teaching* (New York: Longman, Inc., 1983), 58. Used by permission of Longman.

[10]Madeline Hunter and Douglas Russell, "How Can I Plan More Effective Lessons," *Instructor* (September 1977), 74–75. Used by permission of the author, Madeline Hunter. T.I.P. Publications, P.O. Box 514, El Segundo, CA 91245.

ADDITIONAL RESOURCES

Bennett, William J., ed. *What Works: Research About Teaching and Learning.* Washington, D.C.: U.S. Department of Education, 1986.

Bloom, Benjamin S. "The Search for Methods of Group Instruction as Effective as One-to-One Tutoring." *Educational Leadership*, 41 (May, 1987): 4–17.

Brand, Paul, and Philip Yancey. *Fearfully and Wonderfully Made.* Grand Rapids: Zondervan, 1980.

Briggs, Dorothy Corkille. *Celebrate Your Self: Enhancing Your Own Self-Esteem.* Garden City, N.Y.: Doubleday, 1977.

————. *Your Child's Self-Esteem.* Garden City, N.Y.: Doubleday, 1970.

Brownback, Paul. *The Danger of Self-Love.* Chicago: Moody Press, 1982.

Coopersmith, Stanley. *The Antecedents of Self-Esteem.* San Francisco: W. H. Freeman, 1967.

Glasser, William. *Positive Addictions.* New York: Harper & Row, 1976.

Horne, Herman Herrell. *Teaching Techniques of Jesus.* Grand Rapids: Kregel, 1971. A reprint of *Jesus: The Master Teacher*, 1920.

Hunter, Madeline C., and Paul V. Carlson. *Improving Your Child's Behavior.* El Segundo, Calif.: T. I. P. Publications, 1982.

Hunter, Madeline C. *Rx, Improved Instruction.* El Segundo, Calif.: T. I. P. Publications, 1976.

————. *Teach More—Faster!* El Segundo, Calif.: T. I. P. Publications, 1969.

————. "Translating Theory Into Classroom Practice: Elements of Successful Instruction." Motion picture on the planning process. Malibu, Calif.: Special Purpose Films, 1977. (58 minutes, two reels.)

————. Mastery Teaching Video Cassette and Text: *Twenty Modules Designed for Increasing Instructional Effectiveness in Secondary Schools, Colleges and Universities.* Los Angeles: Office of Instructional Development, UCLA, 1981.

Lasley, Thomas J., and Ronald Walker. "Time-on-Task: How Teachers Can Use Class Time More Effectively." *NASSP Bulletin*, 70 (May 1986): 59–64.

Maddi, Salvatore R. *Personality Theories*, 4th ed. Homewood, Ill.: Dorsey, 1980.

McCormack-Larking, Maureen. "Ingredients of a Successful School Effectiveness Project." *Educational Leadership*, 42 (March, 1985): 31–37.

119

McDowell, Josh. *Building Your Self-Image.* Wheaton, Ill.: Tyndale House, 1984.

McWilliams, Shedd, Frank Minirth, and Paul Meier. *Building a Healthy Self-Concept: Video Series.* Richardson, Tex.: Today Publishers, 1985.

Powell, John. *Fully Human, Fully Alive.* Niles, Ill.: Argus, 1976.

————. *Why Am I Afraid to Love?* Niles, Ill.: Argus, 1972.

————. *Why Am I Afraid to Tell You Who I Am?* Niles, Ill.: Argus, 1969.

Rosenshine, Barak V. "Synthesis of Research on Explicit Teaching." *Educational Leadership,* 43 (April 1986): 60–69.

Sanford, Julie P., Edmund T. Emmer, and Barbara S. Clements. "Improving Classroom Management." *Educational Leadership,* 40 (April 1983): 56–60.

Seamands, David A. *Healing for Damaged Emotions.* Wheaton, Ill.: Victor, 1981.

————. *Healing of Memories.* Wheaton, Ill.: Victor, 1985.

————. *Putting Away Childish Things.* Wheaton, Ill.: Victor, 1982.

Chapter 7

Teaching for Learning Styles

In Chapter 3 of this text, learning styles were briefly introduced. Now we will examine how teachers can design their teaching sessions to accommodate the various styles. The work of David Kolb, a scientific researcher in the study of learning styles, is of note, but Bernice McCarthy, who is first and foremost a teacher, makes Kolb's theories applicable to the classroom. The information contained in this chapter will enhance the effectiveness of Christian educators in the classroom when they apply the combined educational principles outlined by Kolb and McCarthy.

Kolb's work, influenced by Piaget's ideas concerning cognitive development, shows the child's progressive ability to think abstractly. If "learning is a continuous process grounded in experience,"[1] and a sequential and unchanging process exists, then Christian educators need to be trained to teach in ways that are appropriate for all the learning styles in order to help learners progress comfortably through the learning process.

The 4MAT System Model in Figure 13 incorporates both the learning styles as well as right- and left-mode processing design. In this system, Quadrant 1 contains those people who are identified by Kolb (see Figure 14) as divergers or imaginative learners. These learners are in touch with the feelings of others and need interaction. Quadrant 2 outlines assimilators or analytic learners. These learners are more comfortable with responding to data or facts. Quadrant 3 describes the convergers or common-sense learners. Convergers use data or facts and desire things to be practical. In Quadrant 4 we have the accommodators or dynamic learners. Accommodators are action-

Figure 13
The Complete 4MAT
System Model[2]

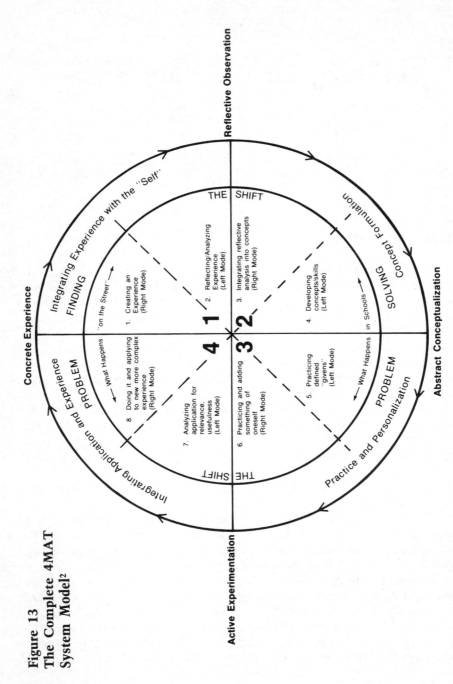

Figure 13. Bernice McCarthy. *The 4MAT System: Teaching to Learning Styles with Right/Left Mode Techniques.* (Barrington, Ill.: EXCEL., 1981), 122. Used by permission of the author.

oriented learners and want to accomplish a task. If, as Christian educators, we believe that children learn most efficiently when they are comfortable and successful in their learning experiences, then we need to design our instruction to provide good learning opportunities.

> The more teachers learn about their own teaching and learning styles, the more they can explain what happens in their classrooms and why. By making explicit their teaching and learning styles, the teachers have taken the first step toward realizing that not all of their students learn as they do; and perhaps problems some children are having result from a mismatch between their teaching styles and students' learning styles.[3]

This will take some conscious planning and work on the part of the teacher, but the results will be worth the effort.

Let's follow this progressive learning cycle through the same Sunday school class situation described in Chapter 6 and see how individual learning styles and brain processing modes are incorporated throughout that session.

THE LEARNER'S ROLE

The text for the lesson is Matthew 20:1–16. The first task that children encounter in the session is to respond to three questions:
1. "What does 'unfair' mean?"
2. "What is the most unfair thing that happened to you this week?"
3. "How did you feel about the unfair event?"

By responding to these questions, we hope to have activated the diverger learning style in a whole brain way. In response to question #2, the diverger should recall a concrete experience involving feelings produced by a real experience, thus activating right-mode processing. By responding to question #3, through reflecting on and analyzing the experience, the left-mode skills come into play.

McCarthy tells us that Quadrant 1 learners need to be involved personally, drawing on their "self-experiences" in order to learn comfortably. This provides them the opportunity to perceive new information concretely, and the question-and-answer format used in the opening minutes of this class session provides them the social interaction they need to process this new information.

Question #1 in the sample lesson is ideal for Quadrant 2 learners because Kolb says that assimilators or analytic learners need to know facts. Being able to define what unfair means engages the left mode's propensity for naming and classifying, but then responding to question #3 causes them to reflect on the experience of applied unfairness. These learners are adept at perceiving ideas and concepts abstractly, but they need to process the information reflectively.[4]

The second event in the lesson on Matthew 20 was to have the children role-play the situation with the landowner and the workers. What happens through this role-play is that Quadrant 2 learners receive more of the factual information they need about the story, but in addition, Quadrant 3 learning styles are also activated. These convergers or common-sense learners, as Kolb identifies them, are only interested in theory when they can perceive the practicality of the theoretical application. The role-play provides the active involvement of the right mode, while responding to the questions provided at the beginning of the lesson engages left-mode processes. Quadrant 3 learners need to actively experiment with situations they have perceived abstractly.

Quadrant 4 learners, those Kolb calls accommodators, are most comfortable when processing concrete experiences through active participation. The role-play provides that forum. By feeling how those laborers felt when they all received the same wage, the accommodator or dynamic learner understands the impact of the story upon people. Through personally experiencing the laborers' dilemma during the role-play, Quadrant 4 learners are able to determine how others might feel in similar situations. Quadrant 4 learners can become catalysts to others' thinking as they project solutions for the resolution of various life dilemmas.

The third event in the class session was the reading of the Matthew 20:1–16 text. This activity helps collect important information for both the Quadrant 2 and 3 learners. Reading the Scripture underscores the reality of the role-play experience.

THE ROLE OF THE EFFECTIVE TEACHER

As learners move around the 4MAT cycle in Figure 13, the role of the teacher also changes. "The primary task of the teacher in Quadrant 1 is to create an accepting climate where the innovative learner (and all types of learners) can explore ideas without being evaluated too quickly."[5] To the opening questions provided in the lesson plan on Matthew 20:1–16, there are no right or wrong answers. The teacher needs only to acknowledge and perhaps restate for clarification the child's response, not evaluate it.

> Please recall that in Chapter 6, one of the characteristics of effective teachers was to be basically nonevaluative and accepting of a child's response.

As learners move into Quadrant 2 of the learning cycle, teachers function in the traditional teacher model of lecturing or giving information. In our class session example, the teacher was giving information both through the role-play and by reading the Scripture.

> Recall that in Chapter 6, effective teachers are task-focused in their teaching.

As the children begin to absorb information by experiencing the role-play and examining the facts of the story through the Scripture reading, they begin to analyze the data and form concepts (depending on the lesson objective) about fairness, about how heaven is the eternal reward for believers, or about God's grace to us.

As children move into Quadrant 3 of the learning cycle, the role of the teacher becomes that of a coach or facilitator.[6] This may be the most difficult role for the traditional teacher to play because the teacher is on the periphery while the learner is center stage. This concept can be illustrated by looking at a basketball team. The coaches are on the sidelines, stressing fundamentals, designing practice, establishing the game plan, and then calling the plays in the game itself. Coaches encourage their players, but they do not supplant the player on the floor. The players have to do the work in order to win the game.

And so it is in the classroom. At some point the learners must actually do the work of learning. The teacher cannot and should not do it for them. The learners must make sense of the learning that is taking place and begin to construct ways to solve the problems presented.

> Recall that in Chapter 6, effective teachers actively involve students in the classroom.

In Quadrant 4 of the 4MAT learning cycle, teachers "create a climate where there is freedom to discover by doing . . . and share it with others."[7] To accomplish this, teachers need to help children evaluate the learning that has taken place and assist them in designing ways to carry that learning into real-life situations. The teacher needs to listen to the learners.

Effective teachers, described in Chapter 6, create a relaxed learning environment and have high expectations for what their learners will accomplish.

LEARNING STYLES AND THE LEARNING PROCESS

In Part I of this text, the learning process was described and substantiated in terms of educational research. In Part II of this text, we have begun to explore the means teachers use to assist learners in the learning process. This comes about as teachers provide input and information for learners to attend to through *listening.* Learners begin to *explore* the teaching concepts as teachers ask questions and students look for information *first-hand.* Learners begin to *discover* truths for themselves as teachers begin to coach, rather than "play the game" for them. The provision of time for student-teacher dialogue, as well as peer interaction provides the climate for *appropriation* of the learning objective. And as teachers help the learners evaluate what has been internalized and make plans to actually do something which alters their behavior, learners *assume responsibility* for what has been learned.

In Figure 14, let's review the applicability of the learning process superimposed on Kolb's characterization of the learning styles. There appears to be compatibility between these two visual descriptions that underscores the need for teachers to learn to teach effectively through all learning styles.

The *diverger* wants to be involved with people but is concrete in his or her approach to learning. Taking in information—**listening**—that requires input from other sources moves the learner toward a more reflective approach that can generate ideas. As learners move into the *assimilator* functions, they can become more abstract and **explore** and **discover** new truths that exist. *Convergers* like to deal with ideas that have practical application and therefore, they are comfortable in **appropriating** and internalizing that which is learned. The accommodator, however, is action-oriented and desires to **assume responsibility** for the learning that has occurred.

The following is a list of suggested teaching strategies designed by Cornett that utilize the various learning styles:

1. Use a variety of questions to stimulate thinking about factual information, drawing implications, and making value judgments.

Figure 14
Meshing Learning Styles
With the Learning Process[8]

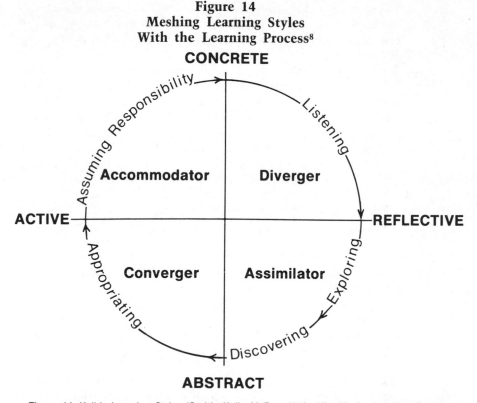

CONCRETE

Assuming Responsibility

Listening

Accommodator   **Diverger**

ACTIVE────────────────────**REFLECTIVE**

Appropriating

Converger   **Assimilator**

Exploring

Discovering

ABSTRACT

Figure 14. Kolb's Learning Styles (Smith, Kolb, McBer, 1986: 16) with the Learning Process (adapted from International Center for Learning, Gospel Light Publication) superimposed. Used by permission of publishers.

2. Create an overview of what is to be learned that provides for the association of past experiences with new ideas.

3. Allow ample time for the learner to process the information and then integrate it by using both right- and left-brain hemispheres.

4. Expect the learners to verbalize at least one new thing at the close of each session.

5. Outline specific expectations when providing listening, viewing, or reading experiences.

6. Provide some type of "warm up" for the lesson.

7. Devise some form of mnemonic technique, such as an acronym or acrostic, to assist in the recall of information.

8. Use visual and auditory means to convey information that will assist the learner in taking in (processing) and recalling (retrieving) information.

9. Use a variety of methods to review and/or reflect on learning, such as role-playing, writing, reciting summaries of the lesson or creating contemporary stories illustrating the learning objective.
10. Rather than simply using praise for a "good job," develop affirming statements that encourage the learner to pursue further knowledge, such as "That is an interesting idea," or "I appreciate the way you did such thorough investigation of the topic."[9]

Valuing a learner's primary learning style and incorporating classroom strategies and activities that use each style in the learning process provides the kind of classroom environment where each learner can be unique but can contribute to the whole.

As teachers respect each learner's contribution to the class, the whole of learning is enhanced. Children begin to feel comfortable, valued, successful, and important to the class. All of these positive, affective attributes influence a child's extrinsic view of self and provides the encouragement to pursue further knowledge with positive expectations.

> Please note the connections made in this chapter between effective teacher characteristics and teaching through the various learning styles.

If teachers desire to teach effectively, they need to concentrate their class preparations on teaching to children who function in each quadrant. The teaching session then becomes an experiential one that incorporates the class into a more wholistic approach to learning.

ENDNOTES

[1]Bernice McCarthy, *The 4MAT System: Teaching to Learning Styles with Right/Left Mode Techniques* (Barrington, Ill.: EXCEL, 1981), 61. Used by permission of the author.

[2]Ibid., 122.

[3]Claudia E. Cornett, *What You Should Know About Teaching and Learning Styles* (Bloomington, Ind.: Phi Delta Kappa Educational Foundation, 1983), 19. Used by permission of the author.

[4]McCarthy, *The 4MAT System*.

[5]Ibid., 127.

[6]Ibid.

[7]Ibid., 127.

[8]Donna M. Smith and David A. Kolb, *User's Guide for The Learning Style Inventory: A Manual for Teachers and Trainers* (Boston: McBer, 1986), 16; and International Center for Learning. Ventura, Calif.: Gospel Light. Adapted by permission from the publishers.

[9]Cornett, *What You Should Know About Teaching*, 29.

ADDITIONAL RESOURCES

Faucett, Robert, and Carol Ann. *Personality and Spiritual Freedom: Growing in the Christian Life Through Understanding Personality Type and the Myers-Briggs Type Indicator.* New York: Image, 1987.

Geller, Lester. "Reliability of the Learning Style Inventory." *Psychological Reports,* 44 (1979): 555–61.

Keeton, Morris, and Pamela Tate, eds. *Learning by Experience—What, Why, How.* San Francisco: Jossey-Bass, 1978.

Keirsey, David, and Marilyn Bates. *Please Understand Me: Character and Temperament Types.* Del Mar, Calif.: Prometheus Nemesis, 1984.

Kroeger, Otto, and Janet M. Thuesen. *Type Talk.* New York: Delacorte, 1988.

Lewis, R. G., and C. Margerison. *Working and Learning—Identifying Your Preferred Ways of Doing Things.* Bedfordshire, England: Management and Organization Development Research Centre, Cranfield School of Management, 1979.

Rosenfield, Israel. *The Invention of Memory: A New View of the Brain.* New York: Basic, 1988.

Talbot, Reg. "Learning Styles in Different Situations." *Creativity Innovation Network,* 9, no. 2 (April-June, 1983).

Webber, Robert E. *Worship is a Verb.* Waco, Tex.: Word, 1985.

Chapter 8

Assisting the Child's Personal Development

In Luke 10:25–28 Jesus underscored the five developmental areas of personal growth. A lawyer asked Jesus the question, "What must I do to inherit eternal life?" Jesus responded using a strategy he frequently employed, that of answering a question with a more probing question, "What is written in the Law? How do you read it?" The lawyer thought about it and then gave the correct answer: " 'Love the Lord your God with all your heart [emotional development] and with all your soul [spiritual development] and with all your strength [physical development] and with all your mind [intellectual development]'; and, 'Love your neighbor as yourself [social development].' " Jesus said, "Do this and you will live."

> *Do this and you will live.* That is a command from Jesus. As Christian educators, we must take seriously each developmental area mentioned in that passage and do our utmost to provide programming in the church that is helpful in all five areas.

We will explore each of the areas and outline ways that teachers and church programs can assist the developmental process. Be aware, however, that even as each area is considered separately, it is difficult if not impossible to isolate the various elements, because they are intertwined in the developmental process.

EMOTIONAL DEVELOPMENT

The church can play a major role in assisting the child's developmental process in positive ways. Healthy emotional development takes place as the unfolding personality develops in accord with a biblical self-image.

The healthy establishment of adult personality takes into account Erik Erikson's emphasis on psychosocial development, which uses four stages during childhood years:

Figure 15
The Childhood Years in Erikson's Stages of Life

Stages	Psychosocial Crisis	Virtue	Radius of Significant Relations
Infancy (Birth to age two)	Trust vs. Mistrust	Hope	Maternal Person
Early Childhood (Ages 2–3)	Autonomy vs. Shame, Doubt	Will	Paternal Persons
Play Age (Ages 3–5)	Initiative vs. Guilt	Purpose	Basic Family
School Age (Ages 6–12)	Industry vs. Inferiority	Competence	Neighborhood, School

Figure 15. Reproduced from *The Life Cycle Completed, A Review*, by Erik H. Erikson, by permission of W. W. Norton & Company, Inc. Copyright © 1982 by Rikan Enterprises Ltd.

Infancy—Birth to Age Two. The Christian education program of the church begins with the nursery. Seldom do leaders in the church realize the importance of this phase in the child's total development. The nursery, which is usually a new family's first contact with a church, needs to be a place where both parents and babies feel secure, safe, and certain that church is a good place to be. The nursery experience sets the tone and the expectations for a child's time in the total program of the church. Therefore, it needs to be a quality experience.

Since according to Erikson, Trust vs. Mistrust are the developmental issues for this period, it is wise to have consistent nursery workers to care for the babies. If it is important for the child to develop hope (the virtue Erikson believes is developed in this stage) that in turn breeds anticipation for future experiences, then what happens to the baby in the nursery must be a concern for Christian educators. The primary care giver for the child during this period is the parent, particularly the mother, and therefore, to have the same people in the nursery caring for the babies is most desirable. With the same care givers there, the infant can expect the same environment, attention, nurturing, and loving response week after week.

The reality in the church nursery is, however, that it usually functions with volunteers who serve a week at a time. For adults, that's a good arrangement. But if the Christian educator is concerned with doing what is best for the child, then nursery workers will be recruited for longer periods, such as one- to three-month periods. Continually changing personnel in the nursery does not offer the infant the opportunities to develop trust or security in the church environment.

Early Childhood—Ages Two to Three. In this stage of child development, the child attempts to establish its own will (Autonomy vs. Shame, Doubt as defined by Erikson). Autonomy develops in children when the significant adults around them are able to affirm their right choices and are firm in redirecting their wrong ones.[2] A sense of self-direction is important to the child during this period. The implication here is not that the child should be allowed to do *anything* he or she desires, but rather that adults offer as much freedom to explore and investigate as is safe and possible.

The Christian education program can provide these freedoms. The physical environment should include interesting, stimulating, and interactive experiences. Children need to be touched, talked to, listened to, loved intently, affirmed, and occasionally redirected in their pursuits.

Play Age—Ages Three to Five. If the child emerges from the first stage with trust in people and environment, from the second stage realizing that personal identity is possible and that self-direction is an option, then the impetus needed to develop Initiative vs. Guilt is present. Erikson states that finding purpose in life is the goal of this stage and it is dependent on the child's ability to imagine who he or she will ultimately become. "The child's identity as a boy or a girl is maximally affected"[3] during this phase and because of this, "emotions and feelings at this stage are genuine, legitimate, and need to be accepted."[4]

Christian educators can provide program experiences that allow children to express their deepest longings. When a child initiates this expression, the teacher needs to accept the efforts without placing value judgments upon what is done or said. Assigning negative labels to a child—"You are a bad girl or boy"—confuses the child greatly, because children at this age are unable to separate the person from the act. These are the kind of experiences that foster an unhealthy development of guilt that can last a lifetime.

The positive bonding that can occur between child, parents, and significant adult role models during this phase can be life-altering and should be handled with caution and care.⁵ Becoming initiators in the world beyond the home is a must for children at this stage, but parents know that dangers lurk and that children still need solid and secure relationships at home.

School Age—Ages Six to Twelve. At this stage, the child's world has expanded to include school, and children are forced into a heightened awareness of others. Children whose basic needs were met as infants learn to trust their environment and those around them. Ideally they move on to become self-directive and apply personal initiative to accomplish their desires. The psychosocial crisis resolved at this stage is Industry vs. Inferiority. Successful achievement during these early stages of life sets the stage for developing the virtue of competence as the child is thrust into an academic climate.

Teachers and students in school and Sunday school now become major contributors to children's views of whether they will do well or poorly in education. Active and participative learning experiences that consciously promote cooperation among the learners, can provide for children the feelings of personal mastery and competence.

It is believed that adequate resolution of the aforementioned dilemmas influence both the child's view of God and self. It is incumbent upon Christian educators to assure that the needs of the child are addressed, thus enabling a fully developed adult psyche to emerge.

SPIRITUAL DEVELOPMENT

In the past, the church has been interested in teaching and training the child in areas of spiritual growth and development at the expense of the other developmental areas. What we know from educational theorists, however, must convince Christian educators that spiritual formation does not occur in a vacuum. Rather, it is integrally woven into the warp and woof of the fabric of life.

Spiritual development is that element within us that hungers for a relationship with our Creator. The fulfillment of that intimate desire is a life-long process or journey that begins in childhood and is the eventual fruit of the mature Christian walk. "That God can be known by the soul in tender personal experience while remaining infinitely aloof from the curious eyes of reason constitutes a paradox best described as 'Darkness of the intellect/But sunshine to the heart'" (Frederick W. Faber).⁶

We are reminded by Lawrence Richards that spiritual formation or faith development is a nurturing process that involves the entire Christian community. Children grow in their faith within the context of the faith community that incorporates nurturing processes of belonging, participation, modeling, instruction as an interpretation of life, and exercising choice in moral matters.[7]

A. W. Tozer states that a relationship with God is not something that comes without deliberate pursuit. It must be "sought by prayer, by long meditation on the written Word, and by earnest and well-disciplined labor."[8] Does that mean that young children cannot begin to "know God" personally? Not at all. The first introduction they have to God is through the relationship with Christian parents and teachers. "One of the basic ways of achieving spiritual growth is through the example of spiritually aware persons."[9]

This is why Christian education is viewed as a partnership between the home and the church. There is constant interaction between the two entities that influences the child's development in all areas. Spiritual development is life-long; we are continually in the process of "be-coming" all that God intended us to be. As we develop, so does our faith.

However, a discussion of spiritual development would be incomplete without mentioning James Fowler's work in developing stages of faith. The structural-developmental theorists, Piaget, Erikson, Kohlberg, and Levinson, laid the foundation for the stage orientation that Fowler uses.

Fowler views the development of faith wholistically and believes his research validates "that human beings are genetically potentiated—that is to say, are gifted at birth—with readiness to develop in faith."[10] Toward that end, Figure 16 merely outlines these stages. Additional resources should be consulted for full descriptions of these stages.

Fowler defines faith as

> imagination as it composes a felt image of an ultimate environment. We image from our experiences of relatedness in the covenantal contexts of our lives. We enter into, form and transform our covenantal relationships in reciprocity with the transcendent backdrop of meaning and power in relation to which we make sense of our lives. As this reciprocal relationship between imaged, ultimate environment and everyday living suggests, faith's imaginal life is dynamic and continually changing.[12]

"Faith begins in relationship. . . . [It is] a way of being, arising out of a way of seeing and knowing."[13]

Figure 16
Fowler's Stages of Faith[11]

1. Undifferentiated Faith (Infancy)

2. Intuitive-Projective Faith (Early Childhood)

3. Mythic-Literal Faith (School Years)

4. Synthetic-Conventional Faith (Young Adulthood)

5. Individuative-Reflective Faith (Young Adulthood)

6. Conjunctive Faith (Mid-Life and Beyond)

7. Universalizing Faith

This attempt to explain the development of faith is of central importance to Christian educators. But Christian educators should read Fowler, as well as those who critique his work, in primary sources to accurately discern his theories and the implications for Christian education.

PHYSICAL DEVELOPMENT

Frequently, church leaders feel that children are at the church for such a short period of time that providing for their physical needs is of little importance. But that is not true. No matter the length of time, physical needs must be addressed if maximum learning is to be expected. The church program should provide an active climate with the kind of equipment, experiences, and environment that will foster healthy physical development.

> Think of a classroom you have visited that felt like a good place for children to be. What was it like? Make some notes in the margin about that room before reading on.

As I travel around doing workshops, in churches, I am always looking for that room (and there are usually only one or two) that meets my criteria for quality classroom space. I look for such things as:

● the size of the room per number of children assigned to it

- the appropriateness of table and chair height for the age level using the room
- where and how the children's work is displayed
- the cleanliness of the room
- the availability and variety of supplies and resources for children's use
- the lighting in the room (both natural and electric)
- the color of walls and furnishings
- the type of floor covering
- how the draperies are arranged at the window (askew or hanging properly).

These elements may seem inconsequential, yet they reveal the energy and care that has been invested in making the room habitable for children.

Active classrooms should be the *modus operandi* in Christian education programs because they enhance and encourage the learning process. This is almost a foreign concept in many churches. Churches seem to be most comfortable with traditional, teacher-centered classrooms, even though educational research is overwhelming in arguments promoting the benefits of more active participation in the classroom. Teachers need to be mobile, moving around the room helping children in a variety of ways. "Teacher mobility is not only essential to facilitate small group and individual work, it is also essential to the spirit of the classroom."[14]

The church should provide tables and chairs, easels, bulletin boards, and chalkboards and place them at a level appropriate for the size of the child using each classroom. A playground on the church premises should be viewed as an extension of the classroom environment. But seldom do churches have playgrounds!

Why are such things needed for the physical development of the child? The development of motor skills is one of the primary tasks of these early years. Children need practice to develop both large and small muscles, and this requires equipment and experiences geared to this need. The church and Christian educators can respond with proper equipment and experiences when they understand the developmental significance of physical activity.

It is unnatural for children to learn while they sit at a table for forty-five minutes at a time. Yes, they need some time for biblical input, but the time should be short (fifteen to twenty minutes maximum), to the point, and then reinforced through activity during the remainder of the classroom time. Young children are active and it is normal for them to run, jump, hop, skip, climb, pedal, steer, throw, catch, bat, and kick (balls, not other children!). Children need both indoor and outdoor equipment that allow them to use and develop these large muscles.

It seems that Christian educators feel they need to apologize to other adults when they seek money for play equipment. Why should this be when we are attending to a child's physical needs, which will facilitate the learning process?

The Christian education program is much more adept at providing experiences for the development of small muscles such as those used in cutting, writing, and coloring. But even here, improvements are possible. Why not provide opportunities for stirring, pounding, dressing, feeding, and bathing dolls; for manipulating puzzles, building with blocks, and molding sand and clay?

Christian educators should address the physical needs of the child and begin a process of purchasing both indoor and outdoor play equipment for the church. Educators know that children have three distinct kinds of play: independent (play by themselves), parallel (independent play but alongside others), and cooperative (coordinate their play with others).[15] Purchase equipment that will encourage all three types of socialization through play. Puzzles, books, and climbing toys are ideal for independent play. Parallel play can be accomplished through riding toys, playing with dolls, and kneading clay or Play-Doh. Cooperative activities could include group games, making cookies or pudding, and playing with a scarf or parachute.

The role of the teacher in providing Christian education through physical activities is to reinforce continually the greatness of the gift God has given us. We are fearfully and wonderfully made, just as Scripture describes, and children need to use their bodies in physically productive ways in the church.

INTELLECTUAL DEVELOPMENT

In order for intellectual development to reach its peak, the other developmental areas must receive attention. The church must begin to approach children and their Christian education wholistically. This will require turning over every stone that might contain an answer to some educational dilemma.

A child's capacity for moral development is linked to his or her cognive determination of judgment and behavior. Piaget's work in cognitive developmental function gave birth to Lawrence Kohlberg's research in the child's development of moral reasoning. How a child reasons with moral issues of right and wrong and what determines his or her ethical decision-making processes are questions that must be continually researched. While much is known about these fields of study, the discipline of Christian education could be furthered by empirical investigation of significant questions relating the influences of home, school, community, church, peers, and society upon moral development. These studies, however, should be conducted with a specific focus upon Scripture and not solely on particular educational theories.

The task for the Christian educator is to know Scripture, and to understand the perspectives presented by various educational theories. Their implementation in the classroom, however, should take place only when the educator can with integrity establish agreement between Scripture, child developmental needs, and theoretical constructs.

SOCIAL DEVELOPMENT

The first contributors to a child's social development are the parents, then siblings, and finally the others in the extended family. It is in the context of the home and eventually the church and the school that personal relationships are cultivated. The product that emerges from these cumulative influences is what social learning theorists refer to as the "socialized individual."

The common roots every child shares do not, however, produce the same result. Although every child has two parents, the homes from which children come can be opposite ends on a continuum. They can be exemplary places for growth or they can be dysfunctional settings—with all the gradients in between.

The relationships through which children become socialized are crucial. God meant for us to be in relationship and to have friends. The fact that God created human beings to share this world with him reveals his relational concept for life. After Jesus recruited and trained the disciples, he sent them out to work together, as associates, in pairs, in relationship to one another (Mark 6:7).

Those who serve children as role models, their peer friendships, and other significant adult influences combine to shape the perception a child will have of life. The cognitive structuralist view of child development says that thinking is not affected by personal relationships, but here is one example of development that occurs not in isolation but as the result of diverse influences.

A child's first view of herself is formed by those around her. The family, the friends, and the teachers who have frequent contact with the child have a tremendous responsibility to allow the child to grow in a loving and trusting relationship, first with the person at hand and then in the intangible relationship with God. The kinds of experiences encountered in growing up, both positive and negative, influence the child.

> Oh, that a magic wand could be waved across the universe that would guarantee each child an environment for personal growth patterned around a loving environment such as that described in 1 John. To love one another deeply, as God first loved us. To know no fear in love; not just to be told we are loved but to sense it, feel it, and know it in the depths of our being through the actions of others.

ENDNOTES

[1]Erik H. Erikson, *The Life Cycle Completed: A Review* (New York: W. W. Norton, 1982), 32–33. Reproduced by permission of W. W. Norton & Company, Inc. Copyright © 1982 by Rikan Enterprises Ltd.

[2]Matthew Linn, Sheila Fabricant, and Dennis Linn, *Healing the Eight Stages of Life* (New York: Paulist, 1988).

[3]Richard C. Sprinthall and Norman A. Sprinthall, *Educational Psychology: A Developmental Approach*, 3d ed. (New York: Random House, 1981), 180.

[4]Ibid., 181.

[5]Donald Joy, *Bonding: Relationships in the Image of God* (Waco, Tex.: Word, 1985).

[6]A. W. Tozer, *The Knowledge of The Holy* (San Francisco: Harper & Row, 1961), 18.

[7]Lawrence O. Richards, *A Theology of Children's Ministry* (Grand Rapids: Zondervan, 1983).

[8]Tozer, *The Knowledge of the Holy*, 22.

[9]Iris V. Cully, *Education for Spiritual Growth* (San Francisco: Harper & Row, 1984), 23.

[10]James W. Fowler, *Stages of Faith: The Psychology of Human Development and the Quest for Meaning* (San Francisco: Harper & Row, 1981), 303.

[11]Ibid., 113.

[12]Ibid., 34.

[13]James W. Fowler, "Faith and the Structuring of Meaning." *Faith Development and Fowler*, Craig Dykstra and Sharon Parks, eds. (Birmingham, Ala.: Religious Education Press, 1986), 16, 19.

[14]David Elkind, *Child Development and Education: A Piagetian Perspective* (New York: Oxford University Press, 1976), 232.

[15]Catherine Garvey, *Play: The Developing Child* (Cambridge, Mass.: Harvard University Press, 1977).

ADDITIONAL RESOURCES

Barber, Lucie W. *Celebrating the Second Year of Life: A Parent's Guide to a Happy Child.* Birmingham, Ala.: Religious Education Press, 1978.

Bushnell, Horace. *Christian Nurture.* Reprint. Grand Rapids: Baker Books, 1979.

Capps, Donald. *Life Cycle Theory and Pastoral Care.* Philadelphia, Pa.: Fortress, 1983.

Chapman, William E. *Roots of Character Education: An Exploration of the American Heritage from the Decade of the 1920s.* Schenectady, N.Y.: Character Research Press, 1977.

Coe, George Albert. *A Social Theory of Religious Education.* Reprint. New York: New York Times, Arno, 1967.

Croft, Dorreen J., and Robert D. Hess. *An Activities Handbook for Teachers of Young Children.* Boston, Mass.: Houghton Mifflin, 1972.

Cully, Iris V., and Kendig Brubaker Cully, eds. *Process and Relationship: Issues in Theology, Philosophy and Religious Education.* Birmingham, Ala.: Religious Education Press, 1978.

Damon, William. *Social Cognition.* San Francisco: Jossey-Bass, 1978.

Enzer, Norbert B., ed. *Social and Emotional Development: The Preschooler.* New York: Walker, 1978.

Gangel, Kenneth O. *The Church Education Handbook.* Wheaton, Ill.: Victor, 1985.

Garvey, Catherine. *Play: The Developing Child.* Cambridge, Mass.: Harvard University Press, 1977.

Gerkin, Charles V. *The Living Human Document.* New York: Macmillan, 1951.

Gesell, Arnold, and Frances Ilg. *The Child From Five to Ten.* New York: Harper & Row, 1946.

Ginott, Haim G. *Teacher and Child: A Book for Parents and Teachers.* New York: Macmillan, 1972.

Glasser, William. *Schools Without Failure.* New York: Harper & Row, 1969.

Groome, Thomas H. *Christian Religious Education.* New York: Harper & Row, 1980.

Herron, R. E., and Brian Sutton-Smith. *Child's Play.* New York: John Wiley & Sons, 1971.

Hunt, James McVicker. *Intelligence and Experience.* New York: Ronald Press, 1961.

Hymes, James. *Teaching the Child Under Six.* Columbus, Ohio: Charles E. Merrill, 1968.

Klausmeier, Herbert J., and Patrick S. Allen. *Cognitive Development of Children and Youth: A Longitudinal Study.* New York: Academic Press, 1978.

Kohlberg, Lawrence. *The Philosophy of Moral Development.* New York: Harper & Row, 1981.

————. "Stages of Moral Development as a Basis for Moral Education." *Moral Development, Moral Education, and Kohlberg.* Brenda Munsey, ed. Birmingham, Ala.: Religious Education Press, 1980.

Levinson, Daniel. *The Seasons of a Man's Life.* New York: Knopf, 1978.

Ligon, Ernest M. *The Psychology of Christian Personality: A Book With a Biography.* Schenectady, N.Y.: Character Research Press, 1975.

Loevinger, Jane. *Ego Development.* San Francisco: Jossey-Bass, 1976.

McCarthy, Melodie A., and John P. Houston. *Fundamentals of Early Childhood Education.* Cambridge, Mass.: Winthrop, 1980.

National Association for the Education of Young Children (NAEYC). 1834 Connecticut Avenue, N.W., Washington, D.C. 20009.

Piaget, Jean. *The Moral Judgment of the Child.* New York: The Free Press, 1965.

Spodek, Bernard. *Teaching in the Early Years,* 2d ed. Englewood Cliffs, N.J.: Prentice-Hall, 1978.

Stone, Jeanette Galambos. *Play & Playgrounds.* Washington, D.C.: NAEYC, 1982.

Westerhoff, John J., III. *Will Our Children Have Faith?* New York: Seabury, 1976.

White, Burton. *Experience and Environment,* Vol. I. Englewood Cliffs, N.J.: Prentice-Hall, 1973.

Wright, J. Eugene. *Erikson: Identity and Religion.* New York: Seabury, 1982.

Youniss, James. *Parent and Peers in Social Development.* Chicago: Univ. of Chicago Press, 1980.

Chapter 9

Managing the Classroom

A group of kindergarten children were lining up to go to the playground. Pausing at the door, the teacher asked, "Can anyone tell me how we are going to treat each other on the playground this morning?" Hands flew up to offer responses. "We aren't going to push each other." "We are going to take turns." "We will be kind." And with those reminders in their heads, they went scurrying out the door for a time of play.

Upon their return, the teacher asked, "Well, how was our time at play?" One chap replied, "Great. We did what we were supposed to do."

This teacher is very wise. She believes in establishing the "rules" for behavior and then expects the children to function accordingly. She knows it is harder for them to maintain classroom courtesies on the playground and that they needed reminders of what was expected of them. In the classroom, she is the enforcer of good behavior. But the playground becomes the proving ground for the classroom training. Outside they are responsible for practicing self-discipline and monitoring their own behavior so that a good time can be had by all.

Managing the classroom inside the church so that quality learning can occur requires teachers to know how to prevent behavior challenges; they must be prepared to deal with any disruption. Maintaining discipline within the classroom helps children learn to respect the rights of others and forms for them an expectation of adult socialized behavior.

147

DISCIPLINE

A concept that must be instilled in Christian education programs is that with activity and freedom in the classroom there is responsibility for self and others. Being created by God with a free will does not exempt the believer from obedience to God. We are independently dependent. Discipline as training, not punishment—is necessary for children to comprehend the order and structure that life requires.

Hebrews 12:11 states, "No discipline seems pleasant at the time, but painful. Later on, however, it produces a harvest of righteousness and peace for those who have been trained by it." Nobody chooses discipline, but it is necessary if believers are to fulfill the expectation of Christ by being everything they were created to be. Discipline is the root word for discipleship. It seems to me that one reason there are so few deeply committed disciples in the church is because adults (teachers, pastors, youth leaders, etc.) have backed away from the scriptural absolutes that Jesus taught.

Classroom management that applies consistent discipline is the responsibility of teachers; it is needed to maintain an atmosphere that is conducive to learning. Children learn self-discipline when teachers take a firm and unwavering stance against disruptive behavior of any sort. The teacher must communicate simultaneously that the child is loved unconditionally, but that love does not require that we accept their every action. Love for the person, however, covers a "multitude of sins" (Prov. 10:12; 1 Pet. 4:8). "You, my brothers, were called to be free. But do not use your freedom to indulge the sinful nature; rather, serve one another in love" (Gal. 5:13).

Training, or discipline in behavior, helps children learn what is appropriate in the classroom, which is actually a microcosm of society. When they are "free to be on their own," then they will know how to be responsible for themselves and others.

Glasser, a pioneer in reality therapy for psychiatric treatment, defines responsibility as "the ability to fulfill one's needs, and to do so in a way that does not deprive others of the ability to fulfill their needs."[1] To allow a child to disrupt the normal classroom routine is not a good thing for the child, the other class members, or the teacher. The methods used to redirect disruptive behavior are a measure of a teacher's classroom management skills.

Traditional teachers pay little attention to redirecting a child's behavior. They control the classroom environment and enforce appropriate behavior with the threat of punishment. They control it through their mere physical size and power. In this type of classroom children are denied opportunities to learn to be responsible for their own behavior.

The reality of adult life is that self-discipline is required to live, work, play, study, produce, and contribute to the society in which we live. Children need to practice appropriate behavior in the Christian education classroom where failure is not critical. Christian educators need to be trained in how to let children be partners in discipline, and ultimately become responsible for their own decisions. Rudolf Dreikurs, a professor of psychiatry, calls this "logical consequences for behavior."

> By using consequences instead of punishment, the teacher allows reality to replace the authority of the adult . . . Consequences permit the child to decide what he [she] can and wants to do about the situation.[2]

What excellent training this is for children as they approach adulthood and assume personal responsibility for decisions they must make!

Glasser has outlined ten steps for maintaining discipline in the *public school classroom*. These steps, outlined in Figure 17, represent an approach to discipline that is not punitive or vindictive, but that requires the teacher to be firm, consistent, calm, and authoritative.

Figure 17
Glasser's Strategy for Maintaining Discipline[3]

1. Teacher asks self: "What am I doing?"
2. If it isn't working, stop doing it!
3. Give recognition to a disruptive student at times when they are not misbehaving.
4. When disruption occurs, ask the student: "What are you doing?"
5. Then ask: "Is it against 'the rules?' "
6. Work out a plan for other alternatives to the disruptive behavior.
7. If infractions continue, isolate the child.
8. The next step is in-school suspension, in the school but out of the classroom.
9. Finally, expel the child.
10. Get professional help for the child if the parents cannot handle the child either.

The complete process is a "tough love" approach to discipline, but when the procedure is followed consistently and thoroughly, it will benefit the child.

This plan may be fine for the public school, but in the church, we do not want to return an unruly child to the home. Christian educators need to pursue all avenues in helping a child remain in the classroom. There are ways Glasser's principles can be applied in church situations.

As a consultant, I was engaged by a very small, urban church to help them administer a vacation Bible school program designed for community outreach. There were some children who attended this VBS only because it was a cheap and convenient baby-sitting service. One such child was Bryan, a sixth grader who knew he was too old for VBS! He came under pressure. His mother commanded that he go.

Bryan was convinced at the outset that VBS was dumb, and he was sure he did not want to be there. Within the first thirty minutes of class, I knew he posed a potential problem that could spread to the rest of the group. So I asked Bryan to accompany me to the hall. There we had a little talk about his behavior. Although he was somewhat passive in his behavior, comments such as "This is stupid," or "Do I really have to do this?" were danger signals. His conversation had to be redirected before his bad attitude rubbed off on the other children.

I adapted Glasser's approach and Dreikurs' logical consequences and worked out a plan with Bryan that I felt might let us all survive the week: I gave Bryan a choice. "Bryan, the teachers here have worked very hard to provide this program for you and the other children. I can see that you have some leadership ability and if you keep up with your remarks about the choices of activities, pretty soon other kids will join you and you all will do nothing constructive. Therefore, you have two choices. You can either participate in the activities provided or you can sit on the bench away from the group. What do you want to do?"

Bryan said, "I'll sit on the bench." I was surprised but said, "If that is your choice, then fine, I'll help you live with it. Whenever you change your mind and decide to participate in the activities, let me know and you can rejoin the group. Until then, you sit on the bench." All this was done calmly and quietly, but firmly.

When we went back into the room, Bryan went to sit on the bench away from the group and I went back to teaching. When the group went outside for play and refreshments, Bryan remained on the bench. This arrangement went on all day Monday. When Tuesday came and Bryan arrived, I said to him, "What is your choice today? Are you going to sit on the bench or participate with the other kids?" "I'll sit on the bench," he said. Surprised again, I said, "Fine, enjoy yourself."

Wednesday, it was the same question and response. Thursday, was a repeat of Wednesday. On Friday Bryan arrived, and before I asked him the daily question, he entered the room and began working on a project. Without comment, he participated appropriately all day. Even at the program that evening he sang the songs and recited the Scripture verses as though he had been integrally involved all week. This was the greatest surprise of all.

Bryan was there all the time in body; he had absorbed all that was going on around him. But I was not going to allow his bad attitude to undermine the whole program. I cared too much about the people, the program, and the children involved to allow one child to disrupt the process for the whole group.

This may sound as if Bryan were being punished. But he was not. He was merely experiencing the consequences of his choice. My role as the adult in the classroom was to help him live with his choice or to help him redirect his behavior. I believe we do children no favors when we permit them to control what is happening in the classroom.

Dreikurs' term for what Bryan experienced is "logical consequences." According to Dreikurs, there are basically four reasons for a child's misbehavior: attention, power, revenge, and a display of inadequacy. Getting the attention of the adult is the single most frequently observed reason for misbehavior.[4] In the foregoing situation, Byran wanted attention. This is why Glasser says that the most critical element in his ten steps in discipline is that of giving recognition or positive attention to a child when the behavior is appropriate. Bryan needed and wanted my attention—and he received it. But I did not allow his need for attention to disrupt the learning environment in the classroom.

Respect, trust, confidence, and faith in childrens' desire to be self-disciplined and responsible for their behavior are precursors to encouraging them to learn. The child is in control of what will be learned. Christian educators need to realize that they can influence a child's learning, but they cannot change it. As believers, we are called to be encouragers of one another. "May the God who gives endurance and encouragement give you a spirit of unity among yourselves as you follow Christ Jesus" (Rom. 15:5). May this spirit of encouragement cause us to honestly evaluate all that we do in the classroom.

EVALUATION

For some reason, the idea of evaluating someone's performance in the church is an abhorrent proposal. Over the years, church leaders have believed that if a person is spiritually gifted in a particular area such as teaching, then training and supervision are not required. I disagree. To have the gift of teaching is desirable, but development of that spiritual gift requires training for one to become effective in the classroom. It takes four years to become a certified public school teacher trained to teach youngsters in such disciplines as biology, mathematics, literature, and music. But all that it takes to teach a group of children in the church is the skill to hold and study a curriculum piece, the ability to inhale and exhale rhymthically, and the inability to say "No."

No matter what size the church is, teacher training is a necessity for the Christian education program to be effective. And if training were to become the expectation for all teachers in the church (and that is a revolutionary concept), then evaluation of their classroom performance and encouragement for them in the teaching process must also be included.

Christian educators as leaders in the church must "have the ability to translate intention into reality and to sustain it."[5] They need to articulate the mission, purpose, and goals of any program. They need to be empowered by the Holy Spirit to recruit, train, and evaluate both the program and the workers for their effectiveness. It is my opinion that without evaluation, people who work in Christian education programs have as much direction as a boat without a rudder! Leaders sit back and wonder why the church has become impotent in its ministry to the world. I believe it is because we have failed to emulate Jesus as the manager of ministry.

Jesus did not train the disciples, send them out to work in pairs and then never observe them in action again (Mark 6:7). In the church though, we seldom train people for their tasks, hardly ever allow them to work in tandem with someone else, and rarely observe or supervise their actual teaching. That is not the model Jesus gave us as leaders. He was continually with his disciples, modeling, instructing, admonishing, and encouraging them. Jesus the leader did not recruit the disciples to fail. He recruited them to a ministry they did not fully comprehend, he trained them for that ministry, cautioned them about the personal cost, redirected their thinking and gave them a glimpse of their ultimate reward for service (Matt. 10–11).

Can Christian educators do less for teachers in the church?

Establish the Criteria for Evaluation. The leaders in charge of a program must determine the part it plays within the total Christian education program. Once that is accomplished, planning should include goal setting. When goals are established on what is to be accomplished through the program, the evaluation of those goals is much easier. Two acronyms, SMAC and SMART, might be helpful for setting goals. They will also help the evaluation process.

S — is it specific?

M — is it measurable?

A — is it achievable?

C — is it compatible (with the overall purpose and other departmental goals?)[6]

or

S — specific

M — measurable

A — attainable

R — realistic

T — timely[7]

After the purpose, goals, and expectations are established, it should be the Christian education administrator who evaluates the teachers and workers within the program. Again, if the criteria for what will be evaluated is determined prior to the actual evaluation, the concerns people might have in being observed and evaluated are alleviated. The purpose for evaluation must be uppermost in everyone's mind: that of doing what we do effectively and excellently for the Lord. "Whatever you do, work at it with all your heart, as working for the Lord, not for men, since you know that you will receive an inheritance from the Lord as a reward. It is the Lord Christ you are serving" (Col. 3:23–24). An excellent example of an evaluation format for classroom teachers can be found in Mark Senter's text, *The Art of Recruiting Volunteers*.[8]

Most workers in the church are dedicated and desire to do their best in their teaching role. The responsibility of the Christian education administrator is not to act as a threat to the teacher's domain, but to evaluate and encourage in a way that affirms their efforts, identifies areas of weakness, and redirects their energies when warranted.

A climate of mutual respect between the Christian education administrator and the teacher is desired. Therefore, Christian education administrators also need to be evaluated by two groups: the teachers they serve and the boards for whom they work. This allows for every element in the Christian education program to be reviewed at least annually.

Evaluate Curricula for the Church. If the church has set one of its goals to be diligent in recruiting, training, equipping, and evaluating teachers and staff, then what they are teaching must also come under scrutiny. There is a wide variety of teaching materials available to churches. The challenge is to effectively review this abundance of curricula to find the most appropriate tools to help teach the textbook of the faith, God's holy Word.

Directions for Evaluating Curricula. The following is an objective method that will assist your Christian education board or committee in making a curriculum selection. Curriculum decision making is often an emotionally charged activity. Using the following approach helps to keep a proper focus on the issues.

1. *As a Board,* review the Statements of Faith and/or Educational Philosophy the publishers have provided. Select those companies whose statements most closely reflect the theological stance of your denomination or church. If you can limit the number of publishers to four or five, the amount of material to review will be manageable.

2. *As a Board,* select some people from the board, some teachers, and a few other interested leaders, and ask them to review the curriculum in the division of their greatest interest and/or expertise. Possible divisions are: preschool (birth to kindergarten), children (grades one to six), youth (grades seven to twelve) and adult (after high school to the grave). Charge them with the task of choosing the most appropriate curriculum for the program under consideration.

3. There are twenty-six criteria for curriculum listed in Figure 18. That is too many to address in a curriculum review. *As a Board,* therefore, select the ten to fifteen criteria you consider to be the most important for your church.

4. *As a Board,* assign a numerical value to each of the criteria you have chosen; ranking them in their order of importance. That means that the criterion most important to you will be assigned the highest number (15, if that is the total number of criteria the Board selected). The least important criterion would be assigned the numerical value of 1.

5. After the curriculum companies have been selected, have *individual reviewers* write their names in the blanks provided at the top of the evaluation form (Figure 18).

6. Each *individual reviewer* should then examine the various curricula to see if they meet the pre-established criteria. For example, your Board has chosen "Christ-centered" (Scriptural orientation) as one of your criteria, and assigned it the top numerical value of 15. Each individual reviewer should determine whether the various

curricula are Christ-centered. If they are, the reviewer would mark a 15 in the appropriate block for each curriculum that meets the standard. The reviewer would continue to judge whether each curriculum satisfied each of the criterion. If it did, the reviewer would mark the numerical value of the criterion in that curriculum's column. If the curriculum did not meet the standard, the reviewer would leave the box blank.

7. When *individual reviewers* are finished examining all the companies under review, the numerical totals in each company's column are tallied. The company with the highest score is the one that in the reviewer's opinion, publishes the curriculum that best meets your *predetermined* criteria.

8. *As a Board*, your task now is to compare the responses of individual reviewers and arrive at a decision based upon their findings. At that meeting, each reviewer can nominate only one publisher—the one that he or she awarded the highest number of total points. If all reviewers nominate the same publisher, then the decision has been made for you. If not, the Board should continue the discussion process *based on the predetermined criteria* until a consensus is reached. When a curriculum is finally chosen it will have strong support because a person's commitment to the final decision will be greater when he or she has actively participated in and influenced the decision.[9]

9. Your new curriculum is the result of the best decision possible at the time, given the information on hand. If the Board accepts the recommended curriculum change, the new curriculum should be used for at least two years before another evaluative review is conducted. Two years will allow for a complete cycle of the curriculum to be used and will avoid a premature decision regarding its effectiveness in your local church.

Selecting curriculum in this manner sets a tone for cooperation among Board members in decision-making, which fosters trust and respect. The spirit of cooperation that exists here can and should pervade the entire Christian education program.

COOPERATION VS. COMPETITION
IN THE CLASSROOM

"Growing up has always been difficult. . . . The boy next to Katie was addicted to methadone at birth. Half the students come from single-parent families. A third qualify for free hot lunches. . . . "[10]

Figure 18
Criteria for Selection of Curriculum[10]

Age Level Reviewed _____

Scriptural Orientation

			RANK

agrees with theology of church
Christ-centered
biblically balanced between Old and New Testament
   stories & concepts
goal—transformation of lives

Educational Components

appropriate for the age level
continuity and progression of content
challenging, motivating & interesting
uses best educational methods
involvement of the learner
deals with life situations

Teacher Assistance

easy to use
resource lists
variety of teaching techniques
room for teacher creativity
philosophy, goals & objectives clearly stated
visual aids available
room set-up suggestions
visuals of acceptable quality
good illustrations
offer more material than can be used
offer teacher training suggestions
provide hints for home involvement

Appearance of the Curriculum

reasonable cost
professional appearance
culturally non-discriminatory

TOTALS

These and many similar statements were recorded in *TIME Magazine* about children growing up in America today.

Children are bombarded daily with issues and behavior they should not have to think about—drugs, AIDS, sexual abuse, divorced families, absent or preoccupied parents, and abusive or uncaring siblings. Where can a child go to be loved and accepted; to achieve and become competent and capable without having to compete with hostile forces?

Certainly not the church. That can also be a most competitive climate.

> Walk into a Sunday school classroom and look around. What do you see?

Almost always, there is the traditional attendance poster with gold stars trailing behind the names of the most frequent attenders. Some classes display charts that record the points a child earns for bringing a Bible and for memorizing Scripture verses. Then there are quiz teams and contests with prizes for those who bring the most visitors or the most money for some worthy project.

Each of these things is actually a competition sponsored by the church, pitting one child against another. There is always one winner and everyone else loses. Just like life in the real world! If you're not a winner, you're a loser and thus, worthless. Each of these seemingly harmless activities can be justified as motivational techniques. But do we want the church to advocate win/lose situations?

Scripture does not support an adversarial or competitive relationship among children (or adults for that matter). Those types of relationships are the creation of the fallen, sinful nature of human beings trying to establish the "pecking order" of society. But the church perpetuates this competitive myth without ever pausing to consider its ramifications for the classroom and children.

God loves every person unconditionally. A child does not have to be first, or the one to have memorized the most verses, or be present each week with a Bible in hand to be "acceptable" in the kingdom. Why do teachers set up these criteria for achievement in the classroom? Jesus taught that servants took the lesser position and yet were honored equally with others (Luke 22:25–27). The greatest in the kingdom are not those who have achieved success in worldly terms, but those who keep his commandments and serve others (Matt. 18:1–10).

I recognize that it is almost un-American to speak against competition, which is the basis for our economic and cultural system. But Christian educators need to seriously examine every activity in the church program and eliminate competitive practices. Social scientists, in hundreds of research studies, have repeatedly decried the negative impact competition has on children and adults. Competition causes destructive stress and even impacts physical health.[12]

Children should memorize Scripture verses in response to God's command to "hide the word in your heart." Must memorization be encouraged by having one child compete against another? Couldn't the group cooperate and learn together? The motivation for memorization should not be a reward promised by the teacher. It should be the intrinsic reward of responding in obedience to God's command.

Cooperation among people must be taught and modeled because it is such a foreign concept to Americans. Jesus did not permit the disciples to work alone or even to think about which of them was the greatest. Being number one in the classroom, therefore, should not be promoted either!

Let us, as Christian educators, be biblical in our approach to the issues that affect classroom management. Let us not adopt the unhealthy expectations of our society and its culture.

ENDNOTES

[1]William Glasser, *Reality Therapy: A New Approach to Psychiatry* (New York: Harper & Row, 1965), 13.

[2]Rudolf Dreikurs and Pearl Cassel, *Discipline Without Tears: What to Do With Children Who Misbehave*, 2d ed. (New York: Hawthorn, 1972), 65.

[3]William Glasser, Filmstrip, "Glasser's Ten Steps to Discipline," (Hollywood, Calif.: Media Fine Film Distributors, 1978).

[4]Dreikurs and Cassel, *Discipline Without Tears*.

[5]Warren Bennis and Burt Nanus, *Leaders: The Strategies for Taking Charge* (New York: Harper & Row, 1985), 226.

[6]Marlene Wilson, *The Effective Management of Volunteer Programs* (Boulder, Colo.: Volunteer Management Associates, 1976), 78.

[7]*Church Building Through Christian Education* (Decatur, Ga.: Presbyterian Church of America, Christian Ed. & Publications, 1980).

[8]Mark Senter, III, *The Art of Recruiting Volunteers* (Wheaton, Ill.: Victor, 1983), 98–99.

[9]M. H. Bazerman, T. Giuliano, and A. Appleman. "Escalation of Commitment in Individual and Group Decision Making," *Organization Behavior and Human Performance*, 33 (1984): 141–52.

[10]Lance Morrow, "Through the Eyes of Children," *Time Magazine*, 132, no. 6 (August 8, 1988): 32–57.

[11]Mary Ellen Drushal, "Attitudes Toward Participative Decision Making Among Church Leaders: A Comparison of the Influences of Nominal Group Technique, Delphi Survey Technique, and Social Judgment Analysis," unpublished doctoral dissertation (Nashville: Vanderbilt University, 1986.)

[12]David W. Johnson, Roger T. Johnson, and M. L. Krotee, "The Relation Between Social Interdependence and Psychological Health on the 1980 U.S. Olympic Ice Hockey Team," *Journal of Psychology*, 120 (1986): 279–91.

ADDITIONAL RESOURCES

Buffington, Perry W. *Your Behavior is Showing*. Nashville: Hillbrook House, 1987.

Campbell, D. Ross. *How to Really Know Your Child: And Help Him Grow into Spiritual Maturity*. Wheaton, Ill.: Victor, 1987.

————. *How to Really Love Your Child*. Wheaton, Ill.: Victor, 1977.

————. *How to Really Love Your Teenager*. Wheaton, Ill.: Victor, 1981.

Chase, Betty N. *How to Discipline and Build Self-Esteem in Your Child*. Elgin, Ill.: David C. Cook, 1982.

Dale, Edgar. *Building A Learning Environment*. Bloomington, Ind.: Phi Delta Kappa, Inc., 1972.

Dinkmeyer, Don, and Rudolf Dreikurs. *Encouraging Children to Learn: The Encouragement Process*. Englewood Cliffs, N.J.: Prentice-Hall, 1963.

Dreikurs, Rudolf, and Loren Grey. *Logical Consequences: A New Approach to Discipline*. New York: Hawthorn, 1968.

Dreikurs, Rudolf. *Psychology in the Classroom: A Manual for Teachers*. New York: Harper & Row, 1968.

Gage, N. L. *The Scientific Basis of the Art of Teaching*. New York: Teachers College Press, 1978.

Glasser, William. *Schools Without Failure*. New York: Harper & Row, 1969.

————. *Stations of the Mind: New Directions for Reality Therapy*. New York: Harper & Row, 1981.

Joy, Donald M. *Re-Bonding: Preventing and Restoring Damaged Relationships*. Waco, Tex.: Word, 1986.

Kohn, Alfie. "The Case Against Competition," *Working Mother* (September, 1987), 90–94.

Walsh, Kevin, and Milly Cowles. *Developmental Discipline*. Birmingham, Ala.: Religious Education Press, 1982.

"What These Kids Need Is . . . " Filmstrip published by International Center For Learning. Ventura, Calif.: Gospel Light.

Wilson, Marlene. *How to Mobilize Church Volunteers*. Minneapolis: Augsburg, 1983.

Chapter 10

Administering
Children's Programs

Leadership in the church is finally receiving the kind of attention it has lacked for decades. Donald McGregor reminds leaders that how people are managed depends on how we view human nature and motivation.[1] Seldom do leaders in the church pause to consider how they manage people. There are some who believe that even to discuss "managing people" is not biblical. But Jesus the "master manager" gave us the model for leadership and management; the art and science aspects of administration. However, this example has been passed over in favor of management models from the business community.

There is much to be learned about leadership, management, and administration in relation to the church. "Church organizations frequently squander the full potential of human resources available to them because they appear to lack understanding, direction or vision, and fail to utilize creatively research findings from the social sciences."[2] Leaders in the church are in a critical position to integrate all that is known from Scripture, managerial theory, and educational practice in supervising teachers.

"Managers are people who do things right and leaders are people who do the right thing."[3] Knowing how to "do things right" directs church leaders back to Scripture to determine what "the right thing" is and how to do it. Administrators in the Christian education program of the church must manage *and* lead.

MINISTERING AS JESUS DID

Of all the managers in history, Jesus had the power, authority, wisdom, and expertise to go it alone in establishing his church, but he consciously chose twelve men to train and empower for leadership. Jesus did not condone the "Lone Ranger" approach to management. He implanted in the disciples' minds an eternal perspective on managing people for a purpose.[4]

Jesus knew the task before him: that of establishing his church (Matt. 16:18). If he was to motivate and involve people in the process, there had to be a vision for them to share, a model to emulate, and a long-term view of the people for whom the ministry was to be conducted.

How did he do it?

His Vision. Jesus maintained a vision for ministry that was to do the will of the Father (John 6:40) in bringing eternal life to believers (John 10:10). This vision became his goal: "My food," said Jesus, "is to do the will of him who sent me and to finish his work" (John 4:34). Even as a child, Jesus knew he had a special calling from God (Luke 2:49) and he knew that each leader to emerge from his earthly ministry would be known by the fruit he or she produced (Luke 6:44).

His Model. In reproducing leadership for the church, Jesus trained his disciples to follow his example to preach, teach, and heal (Matt. 4:23; 9:35; 10:5–8). The disciples were eyewitnesses and servants (Luke 1:2) in this ministry. Jesus often reminded them that he did not come to earth to be served, but rather to serve (Matt. 20:28; Mark 10:45). The disciples were called to be servants as they were being equipped to become the leaders in the early church (Matt. 20:25–27).

Jesus established teamwork as the model for ministry when he sent the disciples and other apprentices out to work in pairs (Mark 6:7; Luke 10:1–2). This shows his desire for us to minister together, to be interdependent both on him and each other (John 15:4–5). The American way is the opposite; to be an individual, not dependent on anyone for anything. Yet Christians must be dependent on God for virtually everything. "To many of us, 'interdependence' suggests that I am not sufficient for myself, that I am dependent on resources beyond my own, that I need other people."[5] This is a fact. Jesus' ministry was relational and he means for ours to be the same. We really do need each other in order to minister effectively.

His View of People. Jesus disdained the leaders of his day who ruled over others with coercive power. Instead, Jesus modeled what has been termed "servant-leadership." Given the carnal nature of human beings, Jesus knew that leaders in the church had to be trained to put the needs and desires of others before their own. "For whoever wants to save his life will lose it, but whoever loses his life for me will find it" (Matt. 16:25). As a disciple following Jesus, the motto became, "So the last will be first, and the first will be last" (Matt. 20:16).

The best test for the quality of modeled servant-leadership is "the care taken by the servant—first to make sure that other people's highest priority needs are being served. . . . Do those served grow as persons? Do they, while being served, become healthier, wiser, freer, more autonomous, more likely themselves to become servants?"[6] What a standard against which to measure one's ministry!

The practice of administering programs for children should have the result that adult workers are better equipped to serve and work together cooperatively within the body of Christ for the glory of God. The Christian education administrator does not need to excel in program design in order to be successful. The attendance records do not need to be the sole measurement of success. Rather, the Christlikeness developed in the teachers and children should be the measurement of success.

> Administrators, take personal inventory. Do you work as a "Lone Ranger" in designing your Christian education programs? Do you delegate responsibilities to capable co-workers without hesitation? Do you know your strengths and weaknesses in regard to ministry? Do you share the decision-making process with others? How many people are currently working with you in the leadership of various programs within the church? Are they growing in their personal commitment and joy in serving Christ as they work with you?

What needs to be considered when servant-leaders desire to initiate a new phase of the Christian education program for children?

DELINEATE THE PURPOSE, GOALS, AND OBJECTIVES OF THE PROGRAM

If the church has a published mission statement, any proposed program within the church should reflect those predetermined priorities. Only recently have churches begun to develop mission statements. The Christian education administrator should not necessarily assume that a church has one. But with or without a definitive mission statement for the church as a whole, children's programming must be consistent with the implied mission.

The Purpose Statement. A purpose statement for each ministry within the church program does not need to be lengthy. Two or three sentences should suffice, but the purpose of the program needs to be set down in advance, because that statement then becomes the driving and evaluative force behind the program. Suppose that your Christian education board desires to establish an after-school program in your church. A purpose statement for this program might be the following: "To provide an atmosphere of Christian caring and love for latch-key children, grades one through six."

This purpose statement defines several ministry aims:

1. "Providing a Christian atmosphere of caring and love" allows for a multitude of activities to take place—instruction, snacks, games, songs, videos, and homework—to name just a few.
2. Targeting "latch-key children" says there is a need for child-care during after-school hours for children of working parents.
3. "Grades one to six" defines the age of the children for which the program is designed.

There is no limit to what could be accomplished in an after-school program with this particular purpose statement.

Goals of the Program. After completing the purpose statement, concentrate on the goals for the program. What are "the ends toward which effort is directed?"[7] Goals are those broad aims that are to be accomplished by the program. Based on the purpose statement for the after-school program above, some goals might be:

- To provide quality child-care for latch-key children;
- To have these children associate the church with meeting their particular needs;
- To provide opportunities for adult, Christian role models to interact with children; and
- To provide both structured and unstructured time for fun and fellowship within a loving environment.

Outline the Objectives. Objectives are "the specific targets we identify that will help us achieve the overall goals."[8] Objectives leading to the accomplishment of the purpose and goals of the after-school program outlined above might be:

- To maintain a ratio of adult workers to children of 1:7;
- To train the adult workers in methods of encouraging personal interaction with children;
- To allow ample time for fun, food, and fellowship among the group;
- To plan the events of each day so they appear as unstructured and free-flowing as possible; and
- To assure the physical safety of children.

Develop Strategies for Accomplishing the Objectives. Establishing the strategies, or the methods for achieving the objectives, is also a necessary component in the planning process. Strategies for accomplishing the objectives might include:

- When the number of children attending is a multiple of five, begin recruiting another adult worker. This will ensure the 1:7 adult-child ratio in the program.
- Conduct training sessions with adult workers using Dreikurs' material. Give adults some educational tools to assist them in encouraging and interacting with children.
- Carefully schedule time to allow children some freedom in the program.
- Train your adult workers in consistent methods for dealing with disruptive behavior.

The planning process is not complete until the Christian education administrator can honestly and forthrightly address each of these phases.

SELECT A TARGET GROUP OF CHILDREN

An after-school grouping eliminates pre-school children and focuses on that segment of your church constituency in first through sixth grades. Determining the target group for the new program helps the leaders to remain focused in providing appropriate activities and content for the group. Even in a program designed for first through sixth graders, there should be three smaller clusters of children: grades one and two, three and four, and five and six. Clustering no more than two grade levels together in a program optimizes the educational value of the program, because the clustering allows for meeting the particular needs of the children within those groups.

The needs, interests, and abilities of first grade children are distinctly different from those of sixth graders. In no way can the disparity between first and sixth graders be overcome within a single group. There are things they can do together, but separate activities also need to be provided.

Clustering children together with more than two grade levels represented, e.g., grades one to three and four to six, will force the teachers to teach to the median grade. The problem then is that children who fall into both the upper and lower grades will have a more difficult time concentrating on the activities planned. Boredom or disruption are likely to result and the value of the program will be diluted.

SCHEDULING THE TIME

One component frequently overlooked in the planning of new programs is time. With an after-school program, setting the starting time for the event depends on when children can be expected to arrive after school. In a rural or urban community where children are bused, it might be possible for the school buses to provide transportation. The church, however, may wish to provide transportation from the school to the church. If children walk home from school and pass the church on the way, the starting time can be earlier in the afternoon. The length of the program and its various components will depend upon your estimate of how much the children can handle at the end of the school day and when parents can pick them up.

Giving prior thought to the time schedule of a new program can sometimes determine the success or failure of the event. The convenience of the adult teachers must also be given consideration, but if elementary-aged children are the target population for the program, it must be offered at a time that is appropriate and feasible for them.

PLAN THE SCHEDULE FOR EACH DAY

Although the after-school program should not appear to the children as being as tightly scheduled as school, some prior planning for each day needs to occur. Producing a program with the outward appearance of little structure requires considerable planning, which sounds like a paradox. The idea is to achieve structure while appearing unstructured. Some items that need to be considered when planning the day are: the fatigue level of the children, their need for a change of pace as they arrive from school, and the expected, if not always necessary, "after school snack."

An outline of the events of the day ("Plan A") with a suggested time sequence should be distributed to all adult workers. This way, everyone knows the plan and who is responsible for each segment. In addition, everyone should know that a "Plan B" might be necessary at any time. Many programs only function with one plan and when something happens that thwarts that plan, the leaders are tossed into panic. The wise Christian education administrator will always have a "Plan A" and a "Plan B" in mind for the day.

Consideration must also be given to budget allotments for the program. Thrift and accountability for funds should be priorities. Stewardship is always important.

EVALUATE THE EFFECTIVENESS OF THE NEW PROGRAM

An integral part of the program should be an evaluation of the program, its workers, the children in attendance, the components of the program, and the effectiveness of the ministry. Examining these elements should send the administrator back to review the initial purpose. Some questions to ask yourself and the committee responsible for oversight of the program are: Is the program accomplishing what it is supposed to accomplish? Which of the goals are being achieved? Are some objectives being ignored in favor of others? What are the greatest strengths and weaknesses of the program? Are there other strategies that could be used in accomplishing the objectives?

Polling the parents and children who are involved in the program is also an excellent way to evaluate its effectiveness. A questionaire for parents might include:

1. If our program ceased, how would you provide this experience for your child?
2. What is the greatest contribution of this program to your family life?
3. If you could change one thing about the program, what would it be?

A questionaire for the children could include such things as:
1. The thing I enjoy most about this program is . . .
2. I really don't like it when . . .
3. I wish someone would ask me to . . .
4. If I wanted to bring a friend to this program I would describe it as . . .

Evaluation is a critical component of planning and designing new programs. It should not be taken lightly nor be undertaken prematurely. But evaluation must take place to assure that the program meets the needs for which it was originally established. Program, personnel, and content evaluation should incorporate all viewpoints and perspectives.

The overriding rationale for evaluation is to uncover those aspects of the program that need to be altered or discontinued. The Christian education administrator is advised not to assume full responsibility or personal glory for any program or project undertaken. One's self-image as a Christian education administrator should not rise or fall on the basis of a program's success or failure. An attitude of detached objectivity, although frequently difficult to maintain, offers greater freedom for the redirection or elimination of specific programs within the church.

ENDNOTES

[1]Donald McGregor, *The Human Side of Enterprise* (New York: McGraw-Hill, 1960).

[2]Mary Ellen Drushal, "Motivational Components of Theory Z Management: An Integrative Review of Research and Implications for the Church," *Ashland Theological Journal,* 18, no. 2 (1987): 8.

[3]Warren Bennis and Burt Nanus, *Leaders: The Stategies for Taking Charge* (New York: Harper & Row, 1985), 21.

[4]Mary Ellen Drushal, "Implementing Theory Z in the Church: Managing People as Jesus Did," *Ashland Theological Journal,* 19, no. 1 (1988): 47–62.

[5]James D. Whitehead and Evelyn Eaton Whitehead, *The Emerging Laity: Returning Leadership to the Community of Faith* (Garden City, N.Y.: Doubleday, 1986), 89.

[6]Robert K. Greenleaf, *Servant Leadership: A Journey into the Nature of Legitimate Power and Greatness* (New York: Paulist, 1977), 13.

[7]Marlene Wilson, *The Effective Management of Volunteer Programs* (Boulder, Colo.: Volunteer Management Associates, 1976), 78.

[8]Ibid., p. 78.

ADDITIONAL RESOURCES

Anderson, James D., and Ezra Earl Jones. *The Management of Ministry.* San Francisco: Harper & Row, 1978.

_____. *Ministry of the Laity.* San Francisco: Harper & Row, 1986.

Block, Peter. *The Empowered Manager: Positive Political Skills at Work.* San Francisco: Jossey-Bass, 1988.

Bruce, A. B. *The Training of The Twelve.* Grand Rapids: Kregel, 1971. Reprint of the 1894 edition.

Cedar, Paul A. *Strength in Servant Leadership.* Waco, Tex.: Word, 1987.

Covey, Steven R. *The Seven Habits of Highly Effective People.* New York: Simon & Schuster, 1989.

Crabb, Lawrence J., Jr., and Dan B. Allender. *Encouragement: The Key to Caring.* Grand Rapids: Zondervan, 1984.

DePree, Max. *Leadership is An Art.* East Lansing, Mich.: Michigan State University Press, 1987.

Dibbert, Michael T. *Spiritual Leadership, Responsible Management.* Grand Rapids: Zondervan, 1989.

Drucker, Peter F. *Innovation and Entrepreneurship: Practice and Principles.* New York: Harper & Row, 1985.

Engstrom, Ted W., and Robert C. Larson. *Seizing the Torch: Leadership for a New Generation.* Ventura, Calif.: Regal, 1988.

Greenslade, Philip. *Leadership, Greatness & Servanthood.* Minneapolis: Bethany House, 1984.

Hersey, Paul. *The Situational Leader.* New York: Warner, 1984.

Kanter, Rosabeth Moss. *When Giants Learn to Dance,* New York: Simon & Schuster, 1989.

MacDonald, Gordon. *Ordering Your Private World.* Nashville: Thomas Nelson, 1984.

Nouwen, Henri J. M. *Reaching Out: The Three Movements of the Spiritual Life.* Garden City, N.Y.: Image, 1986.

_____. *In the Name of Jesus: Reflections on Christian Leadership.* New York: Crossroad, 1989.

Pascarella, Perry, and Mark A. Frohman. *The Purpose Driven Organization: Unleashing the Power of Direction and Commitment.* San Francisco: Jossey-Bass, 1989.

173

Rush, Myron. *The New Leader: A Revolutionary Approach to Leadership.* Wheaton, Ill.: Victor, 1987.

Schaef, Anne Wilson. *The Addictive Organization.* San Francisco: Harper & Row, 1988.

Smith, Fred. *Learning to Lead: Bringing Out the Best in People.* Copublished by Christianity Today, Inc., and Word, Inc., 1986.

Treadwell, William C., and Larry L. McSwain. *Church Organizations Alive!* Nashville: Broadman, 1987.

Youssef, Michael. *The Leadership Style of Jesus: How to Develop the Leadership Qualities of the Good Shepherd.* Wheaton, Ill.: Victor, 1986.

PART III
Relieving Childhood Stress

In Part I of this book, the learning process was outlined and the educational theories supporting it were explored. This is the "WHY" of Christian education. Part II gave insight into the "HOW" of effective teaching. Now we arrive at PART III, a section included "BECAUSE" teachers encounter children with life-altering problems. Remembering our own childhood traumas will sensitize us as teachers to the life situations children face daily. Recognition of children's struggles should send Christian educators and teachers to their knees in regular prayer for the children in their care.

> And just as the infinite love of God enfolds us, so we know that infinite love enfolds all in love, yet it is not our love but the love of God, loving its way, through us, to this world. Would that we could encounter all needs, bear all burdens, dry all tears, fulfill all . . . dreams. But the three-score years and ten close in upon us and the geographical and historical necessities put bounds upon us. Yet in *intention*, we love all, suffer with all, rejoice with all, and laugh with all.[1]

As educators of children, we should intentionally minister to the needs of children. Much of what happens to a child over the years preceding adolescence is no laughing matter. While some things can and should be laughed off, other events demand that adults listen and empathize with the child.

Adult teachers of children cannot always be present when needed but as much as it is possible, listening, caring adults reveal to children the very presence of God.

Chapter 11

Working in Tandem
with the Home

Deuteronomy 6:4–9 reminds us that the home was the original domain of religious education. In the years approaching a new century, however, the modern-day family needs the support of the church in providing such training. Establishing a coalition between the church and the home is no small task. It requires constant concern for the well-being of people of all ages, a ready community of friendly interveners, and a flexible organizational structure that is adequate to meet the needs of today's families.

DEALING WITH CHILDREN IN TRANSITION

Change is inevitable. Some of the changes that take place in children's lives are positive and necessary, but that does not make them palatable. The church, through its people, can assist children and their families in assimilating these experiences.

Moving to a New Neighborhood. It is 8:50 a.m. and the moving van has not arrived. The company representative said it would be there promptly at 8:00—but 8:50 does not seem prompt! Mom cleans up the spilled milk and cereal from breakfast—no small task with three-year-old Susan holding tightly to her leg. As Mother picks her up, Susan clings like flypaper.

"Let's go check and see what Daddy and Bob are doing," Mother says as the two of them make their way through a maze of cartons that contain all the family's earthly possessions. The house that was their home has already taken on an unfamiliar feel. Boxes are everywhere and the shadeless lamps give an eerie appearance to the rooms.

Mom and Susan arrive at the bedroom door and Mother feigns surprise. "Well, Susan, do you believe your eyes? Is that your Daddy with a broom in his hand? And is that your brother holding the dustpan? Wonders never cease," she says as she puts Susan down.

Emptying the dustpan into the last remaining trash bag and examining the clutter being discarded, Mom decides it is typical "ten-year-old-boy trash." There is a crumpled Whitey Ford baseball card (that in better shape would be worth a lot), a dead, black, and hard banana peel, an orange cat's-eye marble, a half-eaten Christmas cookie, and handfuls of cat hair!

The moving van arrives and with it the dreaded moment. The kids, animals, and plants are loaded into the car and the journey into a new life, to a very different place, begins.

When families move all support systems are withdrawn. The comfortable and familiar places and people are no longer there—the doctor who set broken arms, the orthodontist who applied the braces, and the people and places one has grown to trust. The familiar grocery store is no more and the new Main Street, though it has the same name as the old one, looks very different.

"When my anxious thoughts multiply within me, Thy consolations delight my soul" (Ps. 94:19, NASB). That is a comforting verse to which all parents and teachers of children who move might cling. In the midst of the turmoil and trauma of a move the child needs secure relationships and trusted places until the unusual new surroundings become comfortable and familiar. This is an ideal time for the church to begin its work in developing a partnership with the new family. Making Sunday school teachers aware of children who have moved into your area and are visiting class for the first time should be a top priority for Christian education administrators.

Children who have moved need time to settle into their new environment and to find their places among the new faces that surround them. Nursery workers and teachers should be trained to assist children in making these transitions. They need to know that:

1. Calling the child by name, rather than calling, "Hey, you with the green jacket on," is a must for the classroom.
2. Introducing yourself and writing your name for the parent to remember is better than having them call you "The Teacher."
3. Asking an outgoing child in the group to "adopt" the newcomer will assist the newcomer in becoming a part of the group.

Teachers need to be particularly attentive to the unexpressed or nonverbalized needs of the new child and attend to them quickly, thoroughly and without fanfare.

Changing Classes. Whether a family moves because of a divorce, a job assignment, or simply because of a desire to relocate, the inevitable result is that children must change classes. Children, like adults, are uncertain and often fearful when change is introduced.

A move affects children somewhat negatively and promotion Sunday at church can also exact an emotional toll. There are several things that caring adults can do to assist the children in minimizing the trauma of changing classes:

1. Introduce new teachers to the children in advance of the impending move. If the class is moving as a group, then having the new teacher spend some time with them in their current, familiar classroom can be beneficial. You may need to get substitute teachers, but easing the trauma of a move makes this worth the time and effort.
2. If the class is moving as a group, schedule an "open house" in the new room. Parents and children attend together.
3. List the names of all the new children outside the classroom door to assure them that they are expected and that this is where they belong.
4. Provide some time of instruction about the "standard operating procedures" in the new setting.
5. Give a current class member the responsibility for a new child; this will benefit both children involved.

Establishing friendships in the new setting helps a child adopt the new place as home. While friendships cannot be rushed or assigned, a caring teacher can encourage an atmosphere of acceptance and create a place for the new child among those children already there. Asking children, old and new, to share feelings about being in a new place can help sensitize all involved to the difficulties of being "new" and thus ease the transition.

Teachers can help children reach out to others by creating ways to include the new person into the group's activities.

> Creating space for the other is far from an easy task. It requires hard concentration and articulate work. It is like the task of a patrolman trying to create some space in the middle of a mob of panic-driven people for an ambulance to reach the center of the accident. Indeed, more often than not rivalry and competition, desire for power and immediate results, impatience and frustration, and, most of all, plain fear make their forceful demands and tend to fill every possible empty corner of our life.[2]

The classroom teacher must be aware that rivalry, competition, power, impatience, frustration, and fear of change exist among the children in every classroom. How the teacher responds to these sets the tone for acceptance.

Foster Children. A forgotten segment of the population in this country are foster children, who, for whatever reason, are in need of "temporary parents." Imagine the personal panic you would feel at being physically removed from your home and natural parents by a social worker, taken first to a juvenile home, and then moved to a totally new home. No matter how unacceptable the natural home environment is, it is still the child's home. To be removed, even for the most admirable and compassionate reasons, can hardly be explained to a young person.

The age of the child when he or she is removed from the natural home and placed into foster care is a critical element in how well they adjust. Couples who opt for a ministry in foster care should be trained in ways to help the child overcome the potential problems that can occur at critical developmental stages. Couples who agree to become foster parents are to be admired and sought out by the church. Ministry to foster children can be very worthwhile, but the problems are equally great.

How can the church help? By encouraging Christian families to participate in this program, by being supportive of them when children are assigned to their care, and by assisting and accepting the foster children as a vital part of the Christian education program. These are easy things to write, but hard to do.

LOSS AND SEPARATION

A loss that many children encounter in their young lives is the break-up of their parents' marriage. Authorities estimate that one half of all American marriages end in divorce. That statistic fails to describe the strife, turmoil, and trauma that often precedes the actual break-up of a marriage nor the destruction that takes place within the family unit. How does one tell a child that parents are divorcing? The church can help adults know how to address the painful issue.

Teachers must be encouraged to respect the child enough to be honest. Children are resilient and it is easier for them when they know the truth about a situation than it is when they must ferret out what is really happening in the home. Children have an uncanny "sixth sense" that warns them when things aren't as they should be.

Adults must be encouraged not to compound the problem by lying to them.

What children are capable of understanding about adult relationships is very dependent upon his or her developmental age and stage, cognitively and psychosocially. (See Piaget and Erikson's stages of development.) Children absorb reality through the emotional and affective domain.[3] Therefore, "a troubled marriage is very damaging to children, who usually experience problems with their ability to think rationally, logically, and sequentially because of the troubled home front."[4] There are hundreds of thousands of children who live in dysfunctional homes and whose parents settle their differences in the courts. Children are almost always the non-offending victims, but strangely they absorb and assume the responsibility for the dissolution of their parents' marriage.

What a burden for a child to bear! Where does the child have the opportunity to verbalize the fear, the hurt, and the anger that reside within when parents divorce? Often the adults have friends or family who rally around them to support them through the experience, although that supportive relationship should not always be assumed. But who ministers to the child? Usually, *if it is done at all*, it is done by the hurting, angry, and equally fearful parent who remains in the home. This person is the one least likely to be objective, compassionate, and understanding of the child's perspective in the event of a divorce. The church, which has for decades buried its head in the sand to avoid the multiple difficulties of divorce, can no longer avoid the luxury of non-involvement. How would Jesus care for these suffering children?

Christian educators must train their teachers to be aware of signs of emotional stress that frequently erupt into behavioral problems in the classroom. The adults who minister to children must be informed of the situation and cautioned not to gossip or speculate about the causes for the dissolution of the family. When such information is shared, the teacher's immediate response should be to pray diligently for the family and specifically for the child or children involved.

Adults frequently do everything except pray. We need to reverse our instincts: pray first and then minister to the child. Tell the children that you know what is happening at home, that you are praying for them, and that you will be there if they need you.

A teacher's presence, verbally and nonverbally, physically and emotionally, is extremely important to children all the time, but especially so before, during, and after divorce. The family, particularly the children, does not need the teacher's personal assessment of their situation. Jesus said, "Do not judge, or you too will be judged. For in the same way you judge others, you will be judged, and with the measure you use, it will be measured to you" (Matt. 7:1–2). Teachers need to just *be there* for the child, ready to help reassemble life's pieces.

Custody Disputes. It is a terrible dilemma for a child to become a pawn in this very real game of life. For a child who loves both parents, there is no "right" solution in custody discussions. There are only Band-Aids to cover a wound that refuses to heal.

If the divorcing parents are unable to come to an agreement regarding custody of the children, then the courts determine what is "best for the children." When custody is awarded to one parent, the other usually receives visitation rights in some form. But regardless of who decides custody, the children are the innocent bystanders who always lose the most: a parent, an intact home, and the relationships of extended family. What can the church do, and how can Christian educators help? Five things are suggested by researchers: (1) provide emotional support; (2) provide specific information when necessary; (3) provide substitute relationships for those in need; (4) establish the links between the families and professional help; and (5) in the event that professional help is unavailable or its trustworthiness is questioned, provide service in its place.[5]

Again, being available to the children involved in divorce is essential for adults in the church. There is no substitute for "being there" in a time of crisis, whether the crisis is real or imagined. When parents within the church are divorcing, it is usually the senior pastor who ministers to the adults. But the children must not be ignored. They become the responsibility of the Christian education administrator and classroom teachers.

Sometimes a child needs an adult friend or neighbor who will listen and care.

> Ministry of the laity is a state of mind and heart in which what one does is consciously and intentionally neighborly in character. It requires inner strength, courage to persevere, hope invested in a vision not yet realized, and the perspective to question and challenge accepted practice to sustain this ministry; and these are gifts of grace.[6]

Gifts of grace. Where else besides the church can a child be assured these things?

> Recruit teachers for children's programs who genuinely manifest love and concern for children and then make no assumption that they know how "to be present" with the child in a time of need. Train them in ways of "being there."

Death of a Loved One. The pain of loss strikes in many ways and without discrimination. No one is immune. When our phone rang early one Saturday morning, my children were seated at the kitchen table eating their breakfast and overheard only one side of the conversation. But the tone of voice and the words themselves clearly communicated the concern and the message. That's all it took for my children to piece together the other half of the conversation. When the phone was back on the receiver, the immediate response from my oldest child was, "It sounds like I'm about to lose my grandpa."

She was right. Grandpa had suffered a severe stroke and if there was hope of seeing him before he died, we had to act quickly.

When death is imminent, there is no time to explore the five stages of grief—denial, anger, bargaining, depression, and acceptance—nor to determine where you are on the continuum.[7] Instead, there are travel plans and animal care to arrange, calls to make, and options to be considered in the event Plan A or Plan B needs to be employed. The emotions, while ever-present, are repressed to later times.

But soon the memories come—shared ice cream cones, noises Grandpa made clearing his throat in the bathroom every morning, and the joy with which he received the news of becoming a grandparent. Sitting in the back seat of the car were "Good Egg" and "Big Chunk," the endearing names he had called the grandchildren who were now really going to miss him. As president of a college, Grandpa had traveled extensively, but now he was poised for the final journey—the one we selfishly did not want him to make.

As adults, despite all that we know about life and relationships, there is no explanation for what happens in death. Our heads know what is happening, but our hearts ache with pain and loss. The Psalmist says, "Precious in the sight of the LORD is the death of His godly ones" (Ps. 116:15 NASB). We cognitively know that God is with us and has already received that one we loved into his kingdom, but in the midst of funeral preparations, eulogies, food, and relatives coming from near and far, time seems to stand still.

As in the loss of a parent through divorce, who ministers to the child when someone they love dies? Usually, it is the grieving parents, who are also dealing with their own grief process and related issues. How can Christian education administrators and teachers help a child deal with such a loss?

Be There. There is no substitute for physically and emotionally being available to listen to the children. Sometimes adults need to ask questions to encourage the child to talk about the person who has died. Questions like: "What will you miss the most about your

_____ ?" (inserting the appropriate relationship), "Can you tell me about the most fun you ever had with _____ ?"

While these questions may seem difficult to ask, the child needs the opportunity to verbalize inner feelings and memories. A child's ability to respond to these questions obviously depends upon their chronological and developmental ages. No one understands "why" someone dies; we just know that death is a certainty of life.

> Christian educators must be reminded that a close, warm, loving, caring relationship with a child does not emerge at the moment of crisis. The relationship must be developed before a crisis occurs, so that in suffering and bearing one another's burdens, adults have earned the right to ask for and receive responses to unanswerable questions.

Be Honest. Telling a child that the departed loved one is sleeping, on a trip, or passed away is not being honest. Respect children enough to give them accurate responses to their questions. Shielding them from everything involved with death—dying, grave, funeral, and memorial service—really does children no favors. Life is hard. It deals drastic blows now and again, but a part of living and loving is losing those we've loved. While letting go is not easy, it is a fact of life. Everyone feels sad, and tears are healthy and healing. They should not be restrained by comments like, "Big boys and girls don't cry." That's not being honest either.

In all interactions with a child in the throes of a loss, be attentive to their cognitive and psychosocial developmental stages. Young children are concrete and literal in their interpretation of our words. Choose them carefully, honestly, and openly.

Be Aware. In the weeks that follow the loss of a loved one, watch the child for behavior and responses that need attention. Death leaves a sense of vulnerability and can produce a variety of fears. Some children may revert to infantile behaviors, or cling to some trusted adult, or withdraw from contact or discussion with others. Any of these behaviors on a short-term basis should not be alarming. Children need to be reassured that life goes on and that time will ease the pain of loss.

But if these behaviors extend over a long period of time, they can seriously impair a child's adjustment to death and can hinder his or her developmental progress. At this juncture, Christian educators need to help the family find professional counseling for the child.

LOSSES OF ANOTHER KIND

It is a miracle of creation to be born with a body that functions properly. To be born able-bodied and then, because of disease, accident, or deterioration, to become disabled or handicapped brings with it difficult life adjustments.

A broken arm is a temporary disability that will soon heal; casts, complete with the signatures of one's friends, are worn as a "badge of courage." But to be relegated to a wheelchair, to lose sight, or to have one's physical activities severely reduced, causes extreme anxiety and stress for a child and his or her family.

Learning how to cope with a serious disease has an impact on every aspect of a child's life. The simple tasks of getting out of bed, dressing, and climbing into the car that before were accomplished without thought can now become major, exhausting events. Where once there were trips to the "Y" for swimming classes, there are now treks back and forth to doctors and hospitals.

What can the church do to help? It must be sensitive to the feelings of the child and family. It must be creative and include the child in *every* scheduled activity, *regardless* of the logistical problems involved. For example, if a child needs to get around with crutches, braces, or a wheelchair, plan ways for that child to be included in everything with the other children. The term for this in the public sector is *mainstreaming* — moving the child into the least restrictive environment. Accomplishing this takes some preparation and training, but the church needs to be attuned to the needs of these children. Recently, I was in a worship service where the nursery school children were singing a few songs. When the children filed into place, one child who had had surgery and was in a full body cast was carried down the aisle by a teacher. I smiled inwardly at the sight, knowing that here was a church that cared deeply about the participation of *every* child.

Christian educators must remember that the disabled child is first and foremost still a child. The handicapped or disabled child's needs are the same as any other child, and the church should consider how it can help the situation, rather than add to the difficulties.

Family Illness. Children also suffer loss when parents, close relatives, or friends are hospitalized. The uncertainty about the future can shake the very foundations that give a child great security and comfort. As a result of disease or injury, adult disability sometimes occurs. This can also produce mourning and grief in the child, because the parent, friend, or relative can no longer participate in some of the physical activities they once enjoyed together.

Take time to explain to children what has happened and how they can help in the situation. Being needed can be therapeutic and can help in acceptance of the disability. Everyone is affected by these things, and children need to be a part of the discussions about what has happened.

ADULT PROBLEMS THAT AFFECT CHILDREN

Children are frequently innocent victims because they are powerless to alter their situations. They need advocates, Christians who care, who are willing to take up the victims' causes and relieve the stress of daily living.

Financial stress. Have you moved in the last five years? Do you know how much it costs just to pay the initial hook-up fees for the necessities of life: water, electricity, gas, and phone? Have you recently been unemployed? How much fun is it to sit in employment agencies and wait your turn; to stand in long lines to receive your unemployment check; to fill out myriad forms for this or that position? And even with medical insurance, the financial stress on a family when one of its members needs hospitalization and tests is enormous. What stress does a child incur in these circumstances?

Addictions and Abuses. What if a parent has a problem with nicotine or alcohol or cocaine or prescription drugs or pornography or gambling or anything else that is addictive? What if the parent is physically abusive? What amount of stress does the child feel because of his parent's substance abuse?

> A child with an alcoholic father or brother has a 25 percent chance of being an alcoholic, which is five to eight times the incidence in the general population. The probability goes much higher if there is alcoholism in both lines of ancestry. Grandparents as well as parents must be considered, since many hereditary dispositions tend to skip a generation.[8]

What is the responsibility of adults in the church to families in these crises? If the rent is unpaid, the family is evicted. Where do they live? If the parent becomes violent and physically abusive, the children are removed from the home. At what emotional cost is their safety achieved? If the parent participates in illegal enterprises, a prison term is likely the result. What happens to the other family members while the parent is imprisoned? Suppose a parent engages in extramarital affairs, pretending to be concerned about the marriage relationship while exploring others? Are the children spurned and violated by these encounters? Suppose the wayward parent contracts AIDS as a result of these escapades? The social stigma and fear that is attached to these people and their families renders the children helpless victims in a cruel and uncaring world. What would Jesus do?

Sexual and Physical Abuse. The incidence of family violence in the form of emotional, physical, or sexual abuse is a dilemma of staggering proportions. The following statistics from *Newsweek* (December 12, 1988) give an indication of the seriousness and scope of these human atrocities:

- At least 1.8 million women are battered every year.
- Some form of violence occurs in 25 percent of all marriages.
- Twenty percent of women seeking emergency surgical procedures are victims of domestic violence.
- More than 2 million cases of child abuse were reported in 1986, compared with 669,000 in 1976.
- More than 1,200 children die each year as a result of child abuse and neglect.
- Parents who were abused as children are six times more likely to abuse their own children.
- At least 40 percent of all abuse cases involve alcohol or drugs.[9]

In the book *One in Four,* Kepler documents that one in every four children experience sexual assault before the age of eighteen. Kepler states that sexual abuse within a family unit—incest—is estimated to occur in one out of ten families.[10] Can you conceive of the trauma, agony, and anger that is repressed within a child who has been molested, but is not defended or protected? Who does the child hate more, the offending person, or the adult who was aware of the situation and did nothing?

Is all this happening outside the church with no effect on the church? Certainly not. What can the church do for children who are abused? Teachers need to be alert to significant changes in a child's behavior that may signal distress. The observation of the following behaviors should prompt a teacher to probe for possible problems:

- a shift from outgoing behavior to shy, withdrawn behavior (or vice versa)
- regressive behaviors such as resuming thumb sucking or bed-wetting
- discomfort or fear of being left alone with a particular adult or teenager
- precocious, provocative sexual behavior, such as imitating adult sex play (a child will not act out sexually unless she/he has been taught to do so by sexual contact with an adult)
- running away
- drug and alcohol abuse
- nightmares or sleep disturbances[11]

Children are emotional beings and often communicate their deepest needs through their behavior. They need sensitive and caring adults who have enough compassion to look beneath the surface to discover what is happening to the child. Describing the incidence of abuse may be difficult, but it can also be the beginning of healing. "Telling is transformative. When you let someone know what you have lived through and that person hears you with respect and genuine caring, you begin a process of change essential to healing."[12]

Jesus said, "I tell you the truth, whatever you did for one of the least of these brothers of mine, you did for me" (Matt. 25:40). This passage is always viewed in terms of the positive things that are done. Can it be interpreted negatively as well? That is, when we refuse to see what is happening in our world and do nothing (whatever you didn't do for one of the least of these . . . you didn't do for me), have we also done that *against* Jesus?

Jesus compassionately cared for children. Christians need to emulate that model. Christians must remove their blinders and become aware of what happens to children outside of the few minutes they spend in Sunday school and worship. Be prepared to offer children the help they cannot obtain for themselves.

Brothers and sisters in Christ, the church must respond. As Christ's ambassadors to this perverse generation, he has commanded us to go and teach (Matt. 28:18–20). Christian educators and teachers are the closest people to the children in our congregations. Having an *awareness* of children's rights as human beings, being *alert* to symptoms of their distress, giving them the *attention* required to alleviate the situations they encounter, and becoming *active* advocates for their well-being need to be the hallmarks of every Christian education ministry across the country. This should be done without apology or explanation to anyone who might wonder why the church and specifically you, the Christian educator, are involved in the lives of children.

Jesus said, "So in everything, do to others what you would have them do to you, for this sums up the Law and the Prophets" (Matt. 7:12). Christian educators MUST make a difference for children's sake!

ENDNOTES

[1]Thomas R. Kelly, *The Eternal Promise* (New York: Harper & Row, 1966), 30.

[2]Henri J. M. Nouwen, *Reaching Out: The Three Movements of the Spiritual Life* (Garden City, N.Y.: Image, 1986), 72.

[3]D. Ross Campbell, *How to Really Love Your Child* (Wheaton, Ill.: Victor, 1976).

[4]D. Ross Campbell, *How to Really Know Your Child* (Wheaton, Ill.: Victor, 1987), 33.

[5]Donald I. Warren, *Helping Networks* (South Bend, Ind.: Univ. of Notre Dame Press, 1981), 194.

[6]James D. Anderson and Ezra Earl Jones, *Ministry of the Laity* (San Francisco: Harper & Row, 1986), 130–31.

[7]Elisabeth Kubler-Ross, M.D., *On Death and Dying* (New York: Macmillan, 1969).

[8]James E. Royce, *Alcohol Problems and Alcoholism: A Comprehensive Survey* (New York: Free Press, 1981), 149.

[9]Barbara Kantrowitz, Pat Wingert, Patricia King, Kate Robbins, and Tessa Namuth, "And Thousands More," *Newsweek* (December 12, 1988), 59. The sources of this data are "Intimate Violence," Gelles and Staus, 1988; U.S. Dept. of Justice; American Humane Association; National Committee for Prevention of Child Abuse; Edward Ziglar, Yale University.

[10]Victoria Kepler, "Cultural Conditioning Contributes to Sexual Abuse of Children," a paper presented to the Third World Congress of Victimology, San Francisco, July 10, 1987.

[11]Marie Marshall Fortune, *Sexual Violence: The Unmentionable Sin* (New York: Pilgrim, 1983), 169.

[12]Ellen Bass and Laura Davis, *The Courage to Heal: A Guide for Women Survivors of Child Sexual Abuse* (New York: Harper & Row, 1988), 95.

ADDITIONAL RESOURCES

Adams, and Jennifer Fay. *No More Secrets: Protecting Your Child From Sexual Assault.* San Luis Obispo, Calif.: Impact, 1984.

Allen, Roger, and Ron Rose. *Common Sense Discipline: What To Say And Do When Kids Need Help.* Ft. Worth, Tex.: Sweet, 1986.

Berends, Polly Berrian. *Whole Child/Whole Parent.* San Francisco: Harper & Row, 1987.

Berger, Stuart, M.D. *Divorce Without Victims: Helping Children Through Divorce with a Minimum of Pain and Trauma.* Boston: Houghton Mifflin, 1983.

Bibliography: Resources for Persons with Special Learning Needs. National Council of Churches. Office of Special Learning Needs. 475 Riverside Drive, Room 706. New York, NY 10115.

Bissell, Charles B. *Letters I Never Wrote—Conversations I Never Had.* New York: Macmillan, 1983.

Browning, Robert L., and Roy A. Reed. *The Sacraments in Religious Education and Liturgy: An Ecumenical Model.* Birmingham, Ala.: Religious Education Press, 1985.

Buhler, Rich. *Love: No Strings Attached.* Nashville: Thomas Nelson, 1987.

Campbell, Ross, M.D. *Your Child and Drugs: Help for Concerned Parents.* Wheaton, Ill.: Victor, 1988.

Cherne, J. *The Learning Disabled Child in Your Church School.* St. Louis: Concordia, 1983.

Clavell, James. *The Children's Story.* New York: Delacorte, 1981.

Crewdson, John. *By Silence Betrayed: Sexual Abuse of Children in America.* Boston: Little, Brown & Co., 1988.

Drescher, John M. *When Your Child. . . .* Scottsdale, Pa.: Herald, 1986.

Egan, Gerard. *The Skilled Helper: A Systematic Approach to Effective Helping,* ed ed. Monterey, Calif.: Brooks/Cole, 1986.

Elkind, David. *Sympathetic Understanding of the Child: Birth to Sixteen.* Boston: Allyn & Bacon, 1978.

Finkelhor, David. *Child, Sexual Abuse: New Theory & Research.* New York: The Free Press, 1984.

Grollman, Earl A., ed. *Concerning Death: A Practical Guide for the Living.* Boston: Beacon, 1974.

191

Grollman, Earl. *Talking About Death.* Boston: Beacon, 1976.

Hazen, Barbara Shook. *Why Did Grandpa Die?* New York: A Golden Book, 1985.

Holm, Marilyn Franzen. *Tell Me Why: A Guide to Children's Questions About Faith & Life.* Minneapolis: Augsburg, 1985.

Horton, Anne L., and Judith A. Williamson. *Abuse and Religion: When Praying Isn't Enough.* Lexington, Mass.: D. C. Heath, 1988.

Houmes, Dan, and Paul Meier. *Growing in Step: Your Guide to Successful Stepparenting.* Richardson, Tex.: Today Publishers, 1985.

Hyde, Margaret O. *My Friend Has Four Parents.* New York: McGraw-Hill, 1981.

Jackson, Edgar N. *Telling a Child About Death.* New York: Hawthorn, 1965.

Kepler, Victoria. *One in Four.* Mansfield, Ohio: Social Interest Press, Inc., 1984.

Ketterman, Grace. *How to Teach Your Child About Sex.* Old Tappan, N.J.: Revell, 1981.

Kubler-Ross, Elisabeth. *On Children and Death.* New York: Macmillan, 1983.

LaBogardus, Donna. *Christian Education for Retarded Persons.* Nashville: Abingdon, 1969.

Leahy, Robert L., ed. *The Development of the Self.* New York: Academic Press, 1985.

Lester, Andrew, ed. *When Children Suffer: A Sourcebook for Ministry with Children in Crisis.* Philadelphia: Westminster, 1987.

Lickonia, Thomas. *Raising Good Children.* New York: Bantam, 1983.

Malone, Antonia. *Spreading the Light.* New York: Paulist, 1986.

McElroy, Evelyn. *Children and Adolescents with Mental Illness: A Parent's Guide.* Kensington, Md.: Woodbine House, 1987.

McMakin, Jacqueline. *Doorways to Christian Growth.* Minneapolis: Winston, 1984.

Mead, James J., and Glenn M. Balch, Jr. *Child Abuse and the Church: A New Mission.* Costa Mesa, Calif.: HDL Publishing, 1987.

Meier, Paul D. *Christian Child-Rearing and Personality Development.* Grand Rapids: Baker, 1977.

Meier, Paul, and Richard Meier. *Family Foundations: How to Have a Happy Home.* Grand Rapids: Baker, 1981.

Mr. Rogers booklets. *Let's Talk About It.* Family Communications, Inc., 4802 Fifth Avenue, Pittsburg, PA 15213.

Neufeldt, Aldred. *Celebrating Differences.* Scottsdale, Ariz.: Mennonite Publishing House, 1984.

Newman, Barbara M., and Philip R. Newman. *Development Through Life: A Psychosocial Approach.* Homewood, Ill.: Dorsey, 1984.

Nielson, Lindsay A. "Sexual Abuse and Chemical Dependency: Assessing the Risk for Women Alcoholics and Adult Children," *Focus on Family* (Nov./Dec., 1984).

Paterson, George W. *Helping Your Handicapped Child.* Columbus, Ohio: Augsburg, 1975.

Reed, Bobbie. *Stepfamilies: Living in Chrisitan Harmony.* St. Louis: Concordia, 1980.

Roberts, Nancy. *Help For Parents of a Handicapped Child.* St. Louis: Concordia, 1981.

Rogers, Donald B. *In Praise of Learning.* Nashville: Parthenon, 1980.

Rush, Florence. *The Best Kept Secret: Sexual Abuse of Children.* Englewood, Cliffs, N.J.: Prentice-Hall, 1980.

Safford, Philip. *Teaching Young Children With Special Needs.* St. Louis: C. V. Mosby, 1978.

Sanford, D. *It Must Hurt a Lot: A Child's Book About Death.* Portland, Ore.: Multnomah Press, 1986.

Smith, Harold Ivan. *One-Parent Families: Healing the Hurts.* Kansas City, Mo.: Beacon Hill, 1981.

Steinbron, Melvin J. *Can the Pastor Do It Alone? A Model for Preparing Lay People for Lay Pastoring.* Ventura, Calif.: Regal, 1987.

Stunden, Clifford. *How to Raise a Child You Can Live With.* Waco, Tex.: Word, 1986.

Suran, Bernard, and Joseph Rizzo. *Special Children.* Glenview, Ill.: Scott, Foresman, 1979.

Tengborn, Mildred. *Does Anyone Care How I Feel? Family Devotionals to Help Children Understand Their Emotions.* Minneapolis: Bethany House, 1981.

Tips for Teachers Working With Disabled Students. Discipleship Resources. Nashville: United Methodist Church.

Viorst, Judith. *Necessary Losses: The Love, Illusions, Dependencies and Impossible Expectations That All of Us Have to Give Up in Order to Grow Up.* New York: Fawcett, 1986.

Vredevent, Pamela, and Kathryn Rodriguez. *Surviving the Secret.* Old Tappan, N.J.: Revell, 1987.

Wilke, Harold H. *Creating the Caring Congregation: Guidelines for Ministering with the Handicapped.* Nashville: Abingdon, 1980.

PART IV

Pursuing Excellence in Children's Ministry

Patience may be a virtue, but childhood is short and kids need quality ministry NOW! During the 1980s excellence became a rallying cry. In children's ministries, if a program was considered good for children, it should be implemented immediately, with excellence!

> A passion for excellence means thinking big and starting small: excellence happens when high purpose and intense pragmatism meet. This is almost, but not quite, the whole truth. We believe a passion for excellence also carries a price, and we state it simply: the adventure of excellence is not for the faint of heart.[1]

Having "a passion for excellence" is personally costly but the rewards for children make it worthwhile.

The one word that summarizes the emphasis of this section is "PERSEVERE" for the good of the children in your program. Christian educators need to understand "WHY" children learn as they do. They need to know "HOW" to teach effectively, "BECAUSE" children are the beneficiaries of all that is accomplished in the church. Finally, Christian educators need to be encouraged to "PERSEVERE" in the pursuit of excellence because it is so easy to quit or, worse yet, to settle for a mediocre program for children. Children can't know what is best for them and demand it. Children's ministries need dedicated people who are called by God to serve him by working with children.

Chapter 12

Responding to God's Call

When Jesus said to the disciples, "Come, follow me," did they really know what they were doing? Did they understand who "I AM" really was? Did the disciples expect daily sustenance from "the Bread of Life"? We know they had difficulty understanding his teaching through parables, because they frequently asked him to interpret the meanings for them.

In the same way, do adults who say "yes" when asked to serve and teach children really know what they've committed themselves to do? Do they perceive that "doing this unto the least of them" in ministering to children is equivalent to personally serving the Lord? Do educators and teachers understand that their reward will come in heaven rather than at the conclusion of each day's class? Rarely do children leave class and thank their teacher for a wonderful lesson!

The disciples did not initially comprehend their ultimate reward for service or understand what they were to do after Jesus' death. However, Jesus' instructions to them after his resurrection were clear. He appeared to them at least three times and in the final encounter at the Sea of Tiberias; he offered Simon Peter, the beloved disciple who had betrayed him, a full pardon, a reinstatement to ministry, and explicit direction for continued labor (John 21:15–17).

FEED MY LAMBS

Simon Peter was asked by Jesus, "Do you love me?" The reply was, "Yes, Lord." Then Jesus said, "Feed my lambs." *You* (the implied

197

subject of this sentence) have a responsibility to carry through in my absence. He likely meant for the disciples to persevere, even though he was not physically present.

You, as a Christian worker in the church, must *feed* those in your care. The verb *feed* offers multiple mandates for action: "give, provide, serve, produce, supply, minister, support."

Jesus declares his personal ownership of the lambs with the possessive "my." The lambs are his, and educators, teachers, and other workers in the church are his earthly stewards.

The "lambs" in this passage refer to the young sheep, most likely the unweaned ones who were still very dependent on their mothers for nourishment. The lambs could represent young children or young believers. Whatever the meaning of the reference, the responsibility is clear—"Feed my lambs."

TAKE CARE OF MY SHEEP

This second command is Jesus' instruction to persevere in caring for the lambs throughout their growing-up years into "sheephood," or the adult stages of life.

When children mature and move out of the children's division into the youth division of the Christian education program, the teaching/shepherding task is not over. There is much yet to be done to properly care for that maturing lamb, bought with a price by Jesus himself.

Caring for both lambs and sheep does not mean shielding them from every harm they might encounter along the way. Allowing a lamb or a sheep to stray away from the flock to explore the wiles of the world sometimes can teach that sheep invaluable lessons, especially when the sheep returns to the flock (Prov. 22:6).

FEED MY SHEEP

Jesus underscores for a third time in this passage his desire for his followers to persevere in the task they have been given. As lambs grow into sheep, the responsibility of the Christian educator is to continue the teaching/learning process.

Sheep, as adult learners, need feeding and learn in much the same way as do lambs or children. They need to listen, to explore, to discover, to appropriate the discovery, and to assume responsibility for what has been learned. The depth of biblical concepts to which sheep are exposed is different from those for lambs, but the teaching procedures are altered only slightly to allow for the differences in their abilities to discern and absorb the material presented.

PURSUING EXCELLENCE
AFTER RESPONDING TO GOD'S CALL

The old hymn, "Give of Your Best to the Master," rings true when the subject of excellence arises. Because of who he is—Creator and sustainer of the universe, the Redeemer and provider of eternal life— he *deserves* excellence in regard to ministry. And our world depends upon Christian leaders to produce excellence in ministry within the church.

> Our society cannot achieve greatness unless individuals at many levels of ability accept the need for high standards of performance and strive to achieve those standards within the limits possible for them. . . . But those who achieve excellence will be few at best. All too many lack the qualities of mind or spirit which would allow them to conceive excellence as a goal, or to achieve it if they conceived it.[2]

Pursuing excellence as a goal in children's ministry exacts a price from the few leaders who dare to conceive of excellence in designing educational opportunities for children. The price is frequently hard work, and sometimes, work that is not understood by others. That, however, should not deter the Christian educator from pursuing excellence in children's ministry.

> Some people may have greatness thrust upon them. Very few have excellence thrust upon them. They achieve it. They do not achieve it unwittingly, by "doin' what comes naturally"; and they don't stumble into it in the course of amusing themselves. All excellence involves discipline and tenacity of purpose.[3]

Not settling for anything but excellence in children's ministry requires evaluation, redirection, and determination to do everything very well. Nothing should be taken for granted. Every aspect of ministry should be scrutinized for ways to improve and become more effective. "It takes action to achieve excellence—deliberate, careful, relentless action. There are no shortcuts to quality."[4]

But Jesus says, "For my yoke is easy and my burden is light" (Matt. 11:30). "Do you love me? . . . Feed my lambs!" Provide excellent ministry opportunities for children and carry them out intentionally and thoughtfully; without apology to those who do not understand.

DIFFERENCES BETWEEN TEACHING AND EDUCATING

One teacher welcomes a child this way: "Jayne, will you please hurry up and sit down at the table so we can get started with the lesson?"

Another invites a child to participate this way: "Hi Mark. Would you like to work on a puzzle or begin work today by helping Emily put the words of our memory verse in the proper order?"

It is possible to contrast the two approaches here. The first has the teacher functioning as the classroom program director, making sure the students fit neatly into the program. The second has the teacher functioning as a learning coordinator, drawing out of the students their capacities and inclinations for learning.

The second approach is much closer to the concept of *education*. This word comes from the Latin, *educere*, which means "to draw out." The word education suggests drawing out a student or leading a student through a process of learning, growth, and development. In this view of education the adult is more a guide through a learning process than a source of knowledge.

The list below (Figure 19) provides a contrast between two accepted and common views of teaching. As you review this list, add comparisons or contrasts of your own.

Figure 19
Contrasts Between Teachers and Educators

TEACHERS	EDUCATORS
• direct & control every aspect of the class time	• allow choices whenever possible during class
• tell children what they need to do and when	• give some latitude in expected behavior
• know where the front of the room is and stand there	• move around the room to be near any child
• provide samples for what the project should resemble	• offer instruction and guidance for the project, but the finished products may differ

• require children to sit quietly at the table	• allow children to sit, stand or roam
• encourage compliance to stated or unstated rules of behavior	• have broad parameters of acceptability in expectations
• love children but view them as subjects	• love children and view them as fellow-sojourners
•	•
•	•

As an adult, I recently encountered a teaching/learning situation in which my instructor approached me (the learner) as both teacher and educator. A retired pastor in my congregation took me as an apprentice to study the art of stained glass. When I arrived for my first lesson, my "teacher" was ready for me. He had selected a project for me to make and had a sample for me to follow. I chose the glass and when all materials were assembled, he began to instruct me carefully in the sequential procedures: cut out the pattern, cut the glass to match the pattern, grind the glass, surround the pieces with copper foil, solder the pieces together, tin the edges and clean the finished product.

My final exam was twofold: (1) to present my teacher with a list of the steps (and cautions with each of them) that produced a stained-glass work of art, and (2) to give the piece to my best friend and "receive her adoring approval." With his diligent instruction I was able to complete my final exam successfully.

But when I began my second project, my teacher moved into a different relationship, that of an educator. This time I selected both the project and the glass, and there was no sample. The procedures were the same, but I discovered that there were some freedoms or latitudes in how each step could be fulfilled. For example, the glass could be cut all at once or in small sections before moving on to apply the copper foil.

This is a classic example of the distinction between being taught (instructed) or educated (disciplined). Christian educators need to determine what they want to accomplish in the classroom. Do we approach learning as something "to do" or as a skill to help the person "to be"? The response to that question will determine how adults approach children in the classroom.

Christian educators should respond to the following questions:
- Are children objects who need careful supervision, or are they capable of being somewhat self-directed?

- Do children always need a sample of work to be done or can they create around a theme?
- Must children immediately comply with requests, or is there some freedom to accomplish the goal within a reasonable time limit?

The response to *both* of the alternatives contained in each of the questions above is YES. Children do need supervision. They also need to know they are capable of self-discipline. Sometimes they need a sample provided, but they also need to know that creativity is desired and delightful. Children need to be obedient, but adults can view time more flexibly instead of demanding an immediate response.

Children are unique individuals. They have some similar needs, but within that framework, they possess very different personalities, abilities, and experiences of life. Adults in the classroom need to respect children and value both their similarities and their differences. Children need to be taught *and* educated. Each of these verbs elicits a different mind-set and approach to the classroom; one should not be utilized to the exclusion of the other.

ENDNOTES

[1]Tom Peters and Nancy Austin, *A Passion for Excellence: The Leadership Difference* (New York: Random House, 1985), 414.

[2]John W. Gardner, *Excellence: Can We Be Equal and Excellent Too?* (New York: Harper & Row, 1961), 131–32.

[3]Ibid., 92.

[4]Ted W. Engstrom, *The Pursuit of Excellence* (Grand Rapids: Zondervan, 1982), 24.

ADDITIONAL RESOURCES

Dreikurs, Rudolf, M.D. *Social Equality: The Challenge of Today.* Chicago: Henry Regnery, 1971.

Engstrom, Ted. *The Making of a Christian Leader.* Grand Rapids: Zondervan, 1976.

LeTourneau, Richard. *Success Without Succeeding.* Grand Rapids: Zondervan, 1976.

MacDonald, Gordon. *Ordering Your Private World.* Nashville: Thomas Nelson, 1984.

Maxwell, John C. *Be All You Can Be!: A Challenge to Stretch to Your God-given Potential.* Wheaton, Ill.: Victor, 1987.

Swindoll, Charles R. *Living Above the Level of Mediocrity: A Commitment to Excellence.* Waco, Tex.: Word, 1987.

Chapter 13

Meeting the Needs of All Children

Children are a needy segment of the population whose cries for assistance frequently go unnoticed by adults. It is difficult to fathom that children could possibly need anything when one walks into "Toys 'R' Us" or "Children's Palace" and sees the array of available toys. But while these "things" may satisfy their material needs for the moment, their real needs are not met with toys nor entertainment.

CHILDREN NEED TO KNOW

In pursuing excellence in children's ministry, Christian educators need to remember that the single most profound need children have is to be loved, and to really feel it and know it deep inside. In our materialistic world, we err when we allow children to equate the measure of their worth and the degree to which they are loved with how lavishly they are given "things."

In a pilot study that involved adolescents, a researcher asked the group to estimate their collective, monthly, family income. She noted that this question raised more anxiety among the teenagers than the weightier issues explored in the survey. No matter how much a family makes, it is never sufficient to supply all the perceived needs of children and adolescents!

How have children arrived at adolescence with these feelings that finances, no matter the amount, are never adequate? Why is it, on the other hand, that those who were children during the Depression frequently say, "We were poor but we didn't know it"? Why is it that today's children expect their every whim to be met?

Granted, children have tangible needs, but sometimes adults ignore the importance of the intangible necessities of life. These are the roots and foundational principles upon which a disciplined and committed life of service to our Lord and his church grows. The following principles are some scriptural truths children need to understand in order to live life to its fullest.

The Transience of Life. Life as we know it is brief. Whether one lives seven months, seven years, or seventy years, it is never long enough. Scripture reminds us that we are mere shadows and vapors which appear for only a little while (Ps. 39:4; James 4:14). Who we are and what we do during our lifetimes, therefore, are all-important to the kingdom of Christ.

Conversely, Christian educators need to help children develop a long-term view of life that will convince them not to take themselves and the occurrences of daily life too seriously. Sometimes children come home from school with poor grades, or perhaps a bully on the playground has distorted their view of life. On Sunday they might get to church and remember they were supposed to memorize a Bible verse, but they forgot. Naturally, everyone else remembered. These are the kinds of trivial issues that are potentially devastating, unless children learn to take things as they come without overreacting.

Adults need to help children put all of these things into perspective. Helping them identify and weigh what is truly important—and what isn't—is excellent training for adult life. Helping children to laugh at themselves and at the mistakes they make and encouraging them not to dwell on their weaknesses would be significant contributions to a child's long-term welfare. Life is not over if all "A's" aren't achieved. Pride may be injured in being defeated by a bully, but recovery is possible!

Life is too short to be concerned about trivial things. Children need to be in contact with adults who can help them recognize priorities and concentrate on important issues. Piaget's research tells us that young children have difficulty dealing with the concept of time. To them, a week is the equivalent of eternity. Adults need to communicate with children, which means to really *listen* and really *understand* what they are saying. Adults need to help children concentrate on important issues. We don't "have the rest of our lives" to serve Christ. No one is assured of the next breath or of seeing tomorrow. We must get on with the business of "being."

Be Firmly Rooted. "So then, just as you received Christ Jesus as Lord, continue to live in him, rooted and built up in him, strengthened in the faith as you were taught, and overflowing with thankfulness"

(Col. 2:6–7). Children in our American culture need to become a thankful people, firmly grounded in God's Word. At the point in life when a child confesses a need for salvation, we need to thank God for changing the quality of life through the gift of his Son. That is supreme thanksgiving.

But daily thanksgiving for what American children view as small things—life, health, food, education, the provision of God's Word for us, homes, families, and people who care about them—should not be forgotten. It is difficult for children (or adults) to be thankful for something they've never lacked.

Children who have been in the church for a number of years and who have been allowed to "take God and his goodness for granted" have had sown in them the seeds that can grow into adult spiritual mediocrity. Unless Christian educators design ways to keep world issues in the forefront, children have the potential to become spectators rather than concerned participants in the life of the church. A responsibility of Christian educators, then, is to cause children to consider other children around the globe who do not have the certainty of life, health, warmth, compassion, homes, families, or food.

Being firmly rooted in God's Word requires believers to live thankful lives that joyfully, graciously, and generously share from an abundance with others.

Count Oneself Worthy. "With this in mind, we constantly pray for you, that our God may count you worthy of his calling, and that by his power he may fulfill every good purpose of yours and every act prompted by your faith. We pray this so that the name of our Lord Jesus may be glorified in you, and you in him, according to the grace of our God and the Lord Jesus Christ" (2 Thess. 1:11–12).

> Do you believe that people are called into service only when they become adults? Are only adults "worthy of his calling"? Can children serve God even before they can fully understand salvation and all that it means?

When children receive the gift of salvation, they assume a new responsibility in life. They have a new joy as they embark on the process of being prepared to serve Christ and his church. None of this should foster pride within the child. It should foster a sense of desire and availability for the task ahead and it should be encouraged in the child by adult educators. Serving the Lord is serious business and it should not be entered into without humility and a thankful heart of service.

BE GOAL-ORIENTED

" . . . Let us throw off everything that hinders and the sin that so easily entangles, and let us run with perseverance the race marked out for us. Let us fix our eyes on Jesus, the author and perfecter of our faith, who for the joy set before him endured the cross, scorning its shame, and sat down at the right hand of the throne of God" (Heb. 12:1–2).

We are urged to do this because "Jesus Christ is the same yesterday and today and forever" (Heb. 13:8). As children become believers in Jesus Christ, adult educators need to help them "fix their eyes on him," to discover what they are to do in the kingdom, today, tomorrow, and forever. Becoming servants of Christ is not reserved for adults alone. Children have responsibilities too.

Christian educators need to assist children in developing a view of life that will remove the perceived barriers of serving others. Excuses like the following pervade the Christian community and children hear them: "I'm not educated enough to teach a class," or "When I'm finished with my schooling, then I will sponsor the youth group," or "When I get my car paid off, then I'll begin tithing," or "Committee meetings are so boring. Let George do the work." Children are likely to perpetuate the pattern unless some caring adult intervenes to redirect their thinking.

Christian educators have the responsibility for helping children set personal goals of servanthood and simply work toward them. No successful runner ever completes a race while concentrating on the progress of the other runners.[1] If the life task that God has selected for each worthy servant is ever to be accomplished, singleness of mind and purpose must be pursued.

Forgive Oneself. "The end of all things is near. Therefore be clear minded and self-controlled so that you can pray. Above all, love each other deeply, because love covers over a multitude of sins" (1 Pet. 4:7–8).

> Are you perfect? Do you ever make mistakes? What have you done today that needs to be forgiven?

The phrase "love covers over a multitude of sins" carries with it a significant message. When you deeply love someone you can see the good in them, even when they may have done something incredibly stupid (in your opinion)! Jesus said we are to forgive others seventy times seven. Loving others requires that we be forgivers of others' mistakes.

Loving self elicits a similar response. As sojourners (adults or children) in the kingdom, pursuing God's direction and call, we are capable of and likely to make mistakes along the way. We are created in God's image. We are blemished by sin but we are saints in the kingdom because of the sacrifice Jesus paid for us. He forgives our failings. We must also forgive ourselves, pick ourselves up, and continue on the journey laid before us.

CHILDREN WILL NOT ALWAYS BE AS THEY ARE

Every child and adult is in the process of becoming all that God meant them to be. No one ever truly arrives at that ultimate state of development until we meet our Creator face-to-face. Until that moment, we are constantly being perfected.

Figure 20 is a picture of a unique wheelbarrow.

Figure 20
A Unique Wheelbarrow[2]

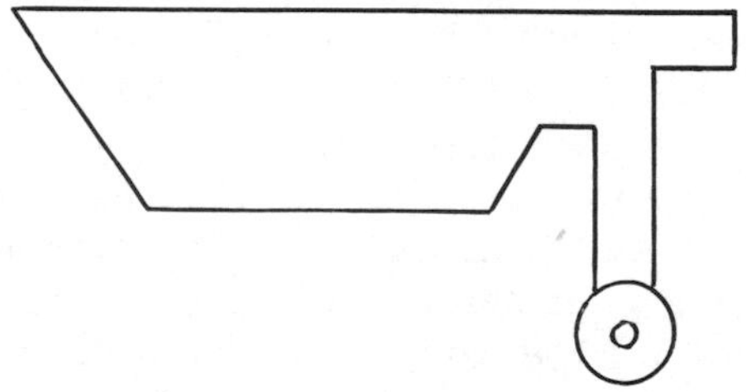

In the space provided below, write five observations you make about the wheelbarrow as it appears.

1.

2.

3.

4.

5.

Of these observations, how many are positive comments? (Fill in the blank.) _____ How many are negative? _____

Most people make negative statements like, "It can't stand on its own," or "It is top heavy," or "It can't carry much load," or "It needs to be redesigned to be functional," or "The tire is in the wrong place." These are accurate statements and reflect human responses to something that isn't exactly as it was expected to be.

Our expectations have an impact on how we view unique wheelbarrows—and children. They can't always stand alone. Sometimes they aren't physically attractive. Their development is such that they are unable to carry the full weight of adult responsibilities. They have adult features and characteristics, but they are not adults. They have not yet fully arrived at adulthood, but they are in the process of becoming an adult. In time they will become adults and assume adult roles and responsibilities. But what we as adults observe about them and say to them largely shapes who it is they become. Children should not have to endure thoughtless, unkind, and negative observations and comments from insensitive adults. A contemporary poster states, "Children are more in need of models than critics." I agree.

Christian education administrators should train their teachers in methods of interaction that permit children to retain their dignity as they develop into adulthood. Dr. D. Ross Campbell, a Christian child psychiatrist, has outlined a four-phase process that, when followed consistently, can help accomplish this goal. He instructs parents that children need eye contact, physical contact, focused attention, and loving discipline in order to develop into healthy human beings who are able to make a contribution to society.[3] How can Christian educators work toward the same goals in the classroom?

Eye Contact. One of the basic principles of communication is maintaining eye contact between the speaker and the listener. This eye contact subliminally communicates that the person is respected, worthy of the necessary time in conversation, and accepted as a valuable member of God's creation. This is also a common social courtesy. Educators and teachers need to look children in the eyes when speaking to them.

Campbell cites research that tells us that eye contact is frequently given to children only when they are being punished. Children also need positive eye contact that is associated with being listened to and cherished.

Physical Contact. Appropriate physical touch is crucial to developing children. Educators can provide this without much effort at all. A reassuring hand on the shoulder, a firm but gentle hug, and a loving pat are all methods for subliminally communicating to children, "I love you, accept you for who you are, and enjoy being with you." Even teachers who have been raised in nontouching home environments can be trained to touch and need to consciously pursue this in the classroom.

Focused Attention. One of the realities of life is that time flies. One moment children are babies in the nursery and in the twinkling of an eye, they are off to college! Educators must be encouraged not to waste class time. There should be a daily goal to have a moment in every session when a single child has the undivided and focused attention of the teacher. Teach the class as a whole but remember that *every* child needs your focused attention.

Time is the most valuable commodity we possess and we all have the same quantity of it per day. You may be asking, "How can I give every child in my group a time of focused attention?" If you *can't* manage it, the student-to-teacher ratio is too high. Recruit other adult workers so that every child has quality time. William Glasser once remarked, "If every child had sixty minutes of sunshine in a week, a time when he or she was the object of an adult's admiration and positive attention, it would markedly influence the child's adult development and perspective." What a simple prescription for adult mental health.

Where can a child be certain of getting quality adult time? At home? Perhaps. In school? Maybe. At a scout meeting? Likely. But the church needs to be at the head of that list for *every* child.

But you say, "If I give every child focused attention, I'll never get through the lesson!" So be it! You will communicate more to the child about unconditional love and acceptance by focusing your attention on them than can be communicated through telling a Bible story. Do not misunderstand: I am not saying that teaching Bible stories is unimportant. Rather, if there is only time to do one of these two important things, opt for the more relational approach to children.

Loving Discipline. Children need the security of knowing what the classroom limits are. They need to experience the consequences of their behavior. We do children no favors when we permit them to control both teacher and classroom. Teachers are in charge, not from a power base but by the authority of their personhood.

Discipline is training in how to conduct oneself in the classroom so that the group is able to accomplish its intended purpose. Without training, limits, and minimal structure, a child is left without moorings that hold him or her to appropriate social behavior.

Jonathan was five. His parents were divorced and he and his mother were living with her parents (Jonathan's grandparents). Grandpa was not thrilled with this arrangement and frequently lashed out at Jonathan verbally and physically. Jonathan was physically large for his age and the rebellion and rage that his parents' divorce had set into motion caused him to be frequently out of control in group gatherings. He sought revenge in the only way he knew how—by hurting other children.

When Jonathan entered a new grade, his reputation preceded him. The teachers expected, and usually were given, multiple disruptions and a variety of misbehaviors. Other children were afraid of him and withdrew from him. In order for Jonathan to function appropriately in the classroom, allow the group to accomplish its purpose, and allay the fears of teachers and children, a single adult was assigned to him. Jonathan was diabetic, very bright, active, loud, and big. He carried around a very deep wound. He cried out to be loved, accepted, and seen as a contributor to something positive in his life.

Jonathan needed intense but loving *eye contact.* He required *physical contact* because sometimes it was necessary to actually restrain him to keep him from hurting himself and others. After some years, the physical touch could be something other than restraint, but first, he had to learn that there were adults at church who cared enough for him that they would not allow him to disrupt every group he attended. He craved *focused attention.* He needed time with adults, particularly males who could serve as quality role models. But most of all, Jonathan needed to learn that society expects a certain degree of *self-discipline* to function successfully with a group of peers. The church program was his only source of these necessities of life.

While attending public school, Jonathan was frequently suspended. At the age of seven, he was unwelcome practically everywhere. The adults at church were going to have to assume the role of shepherd if Jonathan was ever to be trained as a sheep in the flock. He had to be trained to control his inner urges; he had to learn not to vent his personal anger on the smaller, more helpless children around him.

The program for children in the church was the only environment that had the resources, responsibility, desire, and capability to love and train this child into behavior acceptable to his peers. It was not an easy challenge for the adults in the church—his attendance at meetings was perfect! But his adolescent and adult welfare depended on the church workers' ability to persevere with him.

Being able to perceive Jonathan as a fully developed "wheelbarrow," and maintaining the long-term view of who and what he might become, was crucial to achieving these goals.

As Christian educators in the church, we are constantly and for eternity leaving our imprint "on tablets of human hearts." The children who pass through our classes and have contact with us will imitate us. The old phrase that "more is caught than taught" is accurate. Our learners hear our words, they see our actions, they follow our example.

The apostle Peter instructed us that, "Now for this very reason also, applying all diligence,
    in your faith supply moral excellence,
    and in your moral excellence, knowledge;
    and in your knowledge, self-control,
    and in your self-control, perseverance,
    and in your perseverance, godliness;
    and in your godliness, brotherly kindness,
    and in your brotherly kindness, love."
(2 Pet. 1:5–7, NASB)

> We do not teach for a week, or a quarter, or a year, for we are educating for eternity. What does your life teach?

My father-in-law, Dr. J. Garber Drushal, told about his parents' service to the people of Appalachia. He quoted his mother as saying:

> Remember that when we give account of our efforts on the Great Day, we will see there was not much use in writing a book of any kind, unless in it there is that which will inspire those who read it to look at their life work and plan from eternity's viewpoint.[4]

That is my desire for every reader of this text. I pray that as Christian educators, you will adopt an eternal perspective on teaching children, be inspired to serve children with diligence, care about how they learn, and teach accordingly. Be concerned and compassionate as God's tangible ambassador to children.

> You yourselves are our letter, written on our hearts, known and read by everybody. You show that you are a letter from Christ, the result of our ministry, written not with ink but with the Spirit of the living God, not on tablets of stone but on tablets of human hearts. Such confidence as this is ours through Christ before God. Not that we are competent in ourselves to claim anything for ourselves, but our competence comes from God. He has made us competent as ministers of a new covenant—not of the letter but of the Spirit; for the letter kills, but the Spirit gives life. (2 Cor. 3:2–6)

Thanks be to God! Let us go forth and serve children and one another in love.

ENDNOTES

[1]Bruce Larson, *The Great Human Race* (Wheaton, Ill.: Victor, 1987).

[2]David Campbell, *Take the Road to Creativity and Get Off Your Dead End* (Allen, Tex.: Argus Communications, 1977), 9.

[3]D. Ross Campbell, M.D., *How to Really Love Your Child* (Wheaton, Ill.: Victor, 1983).

[4]J. Garber Drushal, *Troublesome Creek* (Lost Creek, Ky.: Joy Sallee Purvis, 1986).

ADDITIONAL RESOURCES

Crabb, Lawrence J., Jr. *Understanding People: Deep Longings for Relationships.* Grand Rapids: Zondervan, 1987.

I Am Somebody! New York: American Bible Society, 1976.

Keating, Kathleen. *The Hug Therapy Book.* Minneapolis: CompCare Publishers, 1983.

————. *Hug Therapy 2.* Minneapolis: CompCare Publishers, 1987.

Montagu, Ashley. *Touching: The Human Significance of the Skin.* New York: Columbia University Press, 1971.

Willard, Dallas. *The Spirit of the Disciplines: Understanding How God Changes Lives.* San Francisco: Harper & Row, 1988.

Zunin, Leonard, M. D., and Natalie Zunin. *Contact: The First Four Minutes.* New York: Ballantine, 1972.

INDEX

Abstract concepts: age and, 77; assuming responsibility as, 91; cognitive development and, 55–56, 121
Abstract learning approaches, 68
Abuse, 157, 186–88
Accommodators, 68, 69, 121–22; brain-processing modes of, 124; learning process and, 126
Addictions, 157, 186, 187
Administration, 163–70, 212; Christ as a model for, 163, 164–65; evaluation and, 169–70; evaluation of, 153–54; purpose, goals, and objectives of, 165–67, 169; schedule planning by, 168–69; target groups and, 167–68; time scheduling by, 168
Adult problems, 186–88
Age: abstract concepts and, 77; assuming responsibility and, 91; discovering and, 67–68; loss and separation and, 181
AIDS, 157, 186
Alcohol abuse, 187
Analytic learners, See Assimilators.
Anticipatory set, 111, 114
Appropriating, 75–83, 90, 91, 93, 113; biblical principles for, 77; defined, 75; educational foundation for, 79–83; learning styles and, 126; practical applications for, 77–79
Art of Recruiting Volunteers, The, 153
Assimilators, 68, 69, 121; brain-processing modes of, 123–24; learning process and, 126
Assuming responsibility, 31, 32, 89–96, 113; biblical principles for, 91–92; educational foundation for, 93–96; learning styles and, 126; practical applications for, 92–93
Auditory learners, 80
Auditory system, 79
Augsburg Press, 65

Barrett, Ethel, 112
Behavioral philosophy, 52; exploring and, 53; listening and, 35; self-image and, 105

Benson, Warren S., 54
Biblical principles: for appropriating, 77; for assuming responsibility, 91–92; for discovering, 63; for exploring, 48; for listening, 30–32
Brain-processing modes: appropriating and, 81–82; learning styles and, 123–24; See also Left-brain modes; Right-brain modes; Whole-brain modes.
Bruner, Jerome, 53

Campbell, D. Ross, 212
Cassette tapes, 32
Changing classes, 179–80
Child-centered curriculum, 54
Children's growth, 211–15
Children's needs, 207–15
Classroom environment, 19, 103–16; accepting biblical self-image and, 105–9; acquiring biblical self-image and, 103–5; lesson planning and, 111–13; lesson preparation and, 113–16; teacher characteristics and, 109–11
Classroom management, 147–58; discipline and, 148–51; evaluation and, 151–55
Cognitive development, 121, 140; assuming responsibility and, 96; exploring and, 54–56; loss and separation and, 181, 184
Cognitive-development approach, 53; See also Structuralist philosophy.
Coles, Robert, 94
Colossians, 48
Common-sense learners, See Convergers.
Communication, 79–81
Competition vs. cooperation, 155–58
Computers, 33
Concrete learning approaches, 68
Concrete operational period, 55
Conditioning, 53
Cone of Learning, 64, 65
Convergers, 68, 69; brain-processing modes of, 124; learning process and, 126
Cooperation vs. competition, 155–58
Cooperative play, 140
Coopersmith, Stanley, 104

Cornett, Claudia E., 126
Counseling, 184
Creativity, 66–67
Curriculums: child-centered, 54; evaluation of, 154–55
Custody disputes, 182

Dale, Edgar, 65
David, 45
Death, of a loved one, 183–84
Deuteronomy: exploring and, 51; on family life, 27; on God's love, 21; on the home, 177
Dewey, John, 53, 54
Disabilities, 185
Disciples, 110, 197; cooperation among, 158; evaluation of, 152; management abilities of, 164
Discipline, 110–11; classroom management and, 148–51; loving, 212, 213–14
Discovering, 61–69, 90, 91, 113; biblical principles for, 63; educational foundation for, 67–69; exploring and, 63; learning styles and, 126; practical applications for, 63–67
Divergers, 68, 69, 121; brain-processing modes of, 123; learning process and, 126
Divorce, 157, 180–82, 183, 213–14
Dobson, James, 104
Dreikurs, Rudolf, 149, 150, 151, 167
Drug abuse, 157, 187
Drushal, J. Garber, 215
Dynamic learners, See Accommodators.

Ebmeia, Howard, 109
Educational foundation: for appropriating, 79–83; for assuming responsibility, 93–96; for discovering, 67–69; for exploring, 51–56; for listening, 33–39
Ego, 94
Eight stages of man, 94–96
Enrichment activities, 47
Environmentalists, 52
Ephesians, 77
Epigenetic diagram, See Eight stages of man.
Erikson, Erik, 93–96, 134, 135–36, 137, 181
Evaluation, 151–55; in administration, 169–70; criteria for, 152–54
Evolutionary thought, 93
Excellence, pursuit of, 199–200, 207
Existentialists, 52
Experimentalists, 53
Exploring, 33, 45–56, 61, 90, 91, 113; biblical principles for, 48; discovering and, 63; educational foundation for, 51–56; learning styles and, 126; listening and, 45, 46; practical applications for, 48–51
Eye contact, 212, 214

Faith, stages of, 137–38
Faith community approach, 18
Families, 106–8; See also Parents; Siblings.
Financial issues, 186, 207

First Thessalonians, 77
Flow of Religious Instruction, The: A Social Science Approach, 62
Focused attention, 212, 213, 214
Forgiveness of self, 210–11
Formal operational period, 55
Foster children, 180
Fowler, James, 137–38
Freud, Anna, 94
Freud, Sigmund, 94

Galatians, 48
Gangel, Kenneth O., 54
Genesis: on innate sinfulness, 34; on likeness to God, 105
Genesis Project, 112
Gesell, Arnold, 52
Glasser, William, 148, 149–50, 213
Goal-orientation, 210–11
Goals, 19–20; of administration, 166, 169; evaluation of, 152–53
God, 52, 105; call of, 197–202; dependence upon, 164; love of, 20–22, 91, 106, 157; self-image and, 109; social development and, 141
Goddard, Henry E., 52
Good, Thomas L., 109
Good Samaritan analogy, 78, 79, 92
Gospel Light Publications, 113
Grief, stages of, 183
Grouws, Douglas A., 109
Guided practice, 112–13

Hall, G. Stanley, 52
Hereditarians, 52
Hewbrews, 148
Hide or Seek, 104
Home, the, 177–88; adult problems affecting children in, 186–88; losses and, 180–84, 185–86; separation and, 180–84; transitions and, 177–80
Humanistic philosophy: assuming responsibility and, 93; exploring and, 52–53; listening and, 33–35
Humphreys, Alice Lee, 22
Hunter, Madeline, 51, 79, 111

Idealists, 52
Illnesses, 185–86
Imaginative learners, See Divergers.
Independent play, 140
Independent practice, 113
Instructional activities, 47
Instructional input, 111–12
Intellectual development, 140–41
Interaction: appropriating and, 78; learning styles and, 121, 123; peer, 126; student/teacher, 212–13
Internalizing, See Appropriating.
Interpretation approach, 17, 18
Intuitive phase, 55
Invariant developmental sequence, 35
Isaiah, 28

James: assuming responsibility and, 93; listening and, 30; on teachers, 112
Jesus Christ, 20; assuming responsibility and, 91, 92; on cooperation, 157, 158; evaluation by, 152; exploring and, 51–52; on forgiveness, 210, 211; goals and, 210; on helping others, 188; as model for administrators, 163, 164–65; as model for parents, 28; as model for teachers, 109, 110, 111, 112; as model of caring, 181–82, 187; personal development and, 133; on responsibility to others, 197–98, 199; self-image and, 108
Jewish tradition, 27–28
Jonathan, 45

Kepler, Victoria, 187
Kinesthetic learners, 80
Kinesthetic system, 79
Kohlberg, Lawrence, 78, 115, 137, 140
Kolb, David, 68, 121, 123, 124, 126

Language development, 29, 38
Learning, See Long-term learning; Short-term learning.
Learning styles, 68–69, 121–28; learner's role in, 123–24; learning process and, 126–28; teachers' role in, 124–25; See also specific styles.
Lee, James Michael, 62
Left-brain modes, 81, 82, 121; learning styles and, 123, 124, 127
Lesson planning, 111–13
Lesson preparation, 113–16
Levinson, Daniel, 137
Liberation approach, 18
Listening, 27–39, 61, 90, 113; biblical principles for, 30–32; defined, 36; educational foundation for, 33–39; exploring and, 45, 46; learning styles and, 126; practical applications for, 32–33
Locke, John, 52
Logical consequences, 150, 151
Long-term learning, 32, 65, 68
Losses, 180–84, 185–86
Love: discipline and, 212, 213–14; God's, 20–22, 91, 106, 157; need for, 207; of self, 211
Luke: on Jesus' confidence in disciples, 110; on personal development, 133

McCarthy, Bernice, 82, 121, 123
McGregor, Donald, 163
Mainstreaming, 185
4MAT System Model, 121, 122
Mears, Henrietta, 113
Misbehavior, 151, 181; See also Discipline.
Mission statements, 165–66
Mnemonic techniques, 127
Moral development, 96, 140–41; See also Spiritual development.
Moving, 177–79

Music, 32, 66

Naturalism, 53; See also Behavioral philosophy.
Neill, A.S., 65
Neo-Thomists, 53
Newsweek, 187
New Testament, 51–52; See also specific books of; specific individuals in.
Nouwen, Henri, 67
Nurseries, 134–35, 177

Oates, Wayne, 106–8
Objectives: of administration, 166–67, 169; lesson plans and, 111
One in Four, 187
Operant conditioning, 53
Oswald, Lee Harvey, 104
Parallel play, 140
Parents, 27–29; administration and, 169; assuming responsibility and, 93; Christ as a model for, 28; emotional development and, 135; illnesses in, 185; listening and, 32; problems with, 157; self-image and, 108; social development and, 141; in times of loss, 183
Paul, 19; appropriating and, 77; assuming responsibility and, 96; discovering and, 63; exploring and, 48
Peer interaction, 126
Personal development, 133–42; emotional development and, 134–36; intellectual development and, 140–41; physical development and, 138–40; social development and, 141–42; spiritual development and, 136–38
Peter, See Simon Peter.
Peterson, Michael, 52, 53
Philosophy of Education: Issues and Options, 52
Physical contact, 212–13, 214
Physical development, 138–40
Piaget, Jean, 53, 54–56, 67–68, 77, 81, 121, 137, 140, 181, 208
Plato, 108
Play, 94, 140
Practical applications: for appropriating, 77–79; for assuming responsibility, 92–93; for discovery, 63–67; educational foundation for, See Educational foundation.; for exploring, 48–51; for listening, 32–33
Practice, 112–13
Prayer: lesson preparation and, 113, 116; loss and separation and, 181
Preconceptual phase, 55
Problem solving abilities, 38
Psychoanalysis, 94
Psychoanalytic approach, 52; See also Humanistic philosophy.
Psychosexual development, 93, 96

Psychosocial development, 134, 135–36; assuming responsibility and, 93–96; loss and separation and, 184
Public schools, discipline in, 149, 150
Punishment, 212; vs. discipline, 148
Purpose: of administration, 165–66, 169; lesson plans and, 111

Questioning: appropriating and, 79; learning styles and, 126

Reading abilities, 29, 32, 38, 39
Reasoning abilities, 38, 39
Reinforcement, 115; conditioned, 53; listening and, 35
Religious instruction approach, 18
Representational systems, 79–81
Responsibility, See Assuming responsibility.
Richards, Lawrence, 137
Right-brain modes, 81, 82, 121; learning styles and, 123, 124, 127
Role models: Christ as, See under Jesus Christ.; for social development, 141; teachers as, 112
Role-playing, 114, 125; learning styles and, 124, 128

Schedule planning, 168–69
Second Corinthians: discovering and, 63; listening and, 30
Self-discipline, 202, 214; assuming responsibility and, 92–93; classroom management and, 147; listening and, 35
Self-esteem, 104
Self-image, biblical: accepting, 105–9; acquiring, 103–5; emotional development and, 134
Self-worth, 209
Sensomotor period, 54–55
Senter, Mark, 153
Separation, 180–84
Sexual abuse, 157, 187–88
Short-term learning, 31, 90–91
Siblings: problems with, 157; social development and, 141
Simon Peter, 197, 215
Skinner, B.F., 52, 53
SMAC, 153
SMART, 153
Social behavior, 29

Social learning theory, 53, 141; See also Behavioral philosophy.
Speech development, 29
Spiritual development, 136–38; See also Moral development.
Spiritual development approach, 17, 18
Stott, John R.W., 115–16
Structuralist philosophy: exploring and, 53–56; listening and, 35–36
Summerhill Farm, 65

Target groups, 167–68
Teacher-centered classrooms, 139
Teachers, 19, 28–29; appropriating and, 78–81; characteristics of effective, 109–11; communication and, 79–81; contrast between educators and, 200–202; dealing with abuse, 187–88; discipline and, 148–49; discovering and, 62, 67, 68–69; evaluation of, 151–53; exploring and, 45, 46–47, 48, 49, 50–51; interaction of with children, 212–13; learning styles and, 68–69, 124–25, 126, 128; lesson planning and, 111–13; lesson preparation and, 113–16; listening and, 30–31, 32, 33–34, 35, 36; losses and, 180–82, 183–84; physical development and, 139, 140; as role models, 112; self-image and, 108; training of, 151–52; transitions and, 178–80
Terman, Lewis, 52
Time: generosity with, 213; scheduling of, 168
Time Magazine, 157
Tithing, 31–32, 76–77
Tough love, 149
Tozer, A. W., 137
Transitions, 177–80

Understanding, checking for, 112

Video tapes, 33
Visual learners, 79, 80
Visual system, 79

Watson, John B., 52
Whole-brain modes, 81, 123
Wholistic approach: to exploring, 51, 52; to intellectual development, 140; learning styles and, 128; to spiritual development, 137